MKLM Library

ENCYCLICAL LETTER
REDEMPTORIS MISSIO
OF THE SUPREME PONTIFF

JOHN PAUL II
ON THE
PERMANENT VALIDITY
OF THE
CHURCH'S MISSIONARY MANDATE

BOOKS & MEDIA
BOSTON

Vatican Translation

ISBN 0-8198-4746-1

Printed and published in the U.S.A. by Pauline Books & Media,
50 Saint Pauls Avenue, Boston MA 02130-3491.

www.pauline.org

Pauline Books & Media is the publishing house of the Daughters
of St. Paul, an international congregation of women religious
serving the Church with the communications media.

4 5 6 7 8 9   04 03 02 01 00 99

Contents

Venerable Brothers,
Beloved Sons and Daughters,
Health and the Apostolic Blessing!

Introduction

1. The mission of Christ the Redeemer, which is entrusted to the Church, is still very far from completion. As the second millennium after Christ's coming draws to an end, an overall view of the human race shows that this mission is still only beginning and that we must commit ourselves wholeheartedly to its service. It is the Spirit who impels us to proclaim the great works of God: "For if I preach the Gospel, that gives me no ground for boasting. For necessity is laid upon me. Woe to me if I do not preach the Gospel!" (1 Cor 9:16)

In the name of the whole Church, I sense an urgent duty to repeat this cry of St. Paul. From the beginning of my Pontificate I have chosen to travel to the ends of the earth in order to show this missionary concern. My direct contact with peoples who do not know Christ has convinced me even more of the *urgency of missionary activity,* a subject to which I am devoting the present encyclical.

The Second Vatican Council sought to renew the Church's life and activity in the light of the needs of the contemporary world. The Council emphasized the Church's "missionary nature," basing it in a dynamic way on the Trinitarian mission itself. The missionary thrust therefore belongs to the very nature of the Christian life, and is also the inspiration behind ecumenism: "that they may all be one...so that the world may believe that you have sent me" (Jn 17:21).

2. The Council has already borne much fruit in the realm of missionary activity. There has been an increase of local churches with their own bishops, clergy and workers in the apostolate. The presence of Christian communities is more evident in the life of nations, and communion between the churches has led to a lively exchange of spiritual benefits and gifts. The commitment of the laity to the work of evangelization is changing ecclesial life, while particular churches are more willing to meet with the members of other Christian churches and other religions, and to enter into dialogue and cooperation with them. Above all, there is a new awareness that *missionary activity is a matter for all Christians*, for all dioceses and parishes, Church institutions and associations.

Nevertheless, in this "new springtime" of Christianity there is an undeniable negative tendency, and the present document is meant to help overcome it. Missionary activity specifically directed "to the nations" *(ad gentes)* appears to be waning, and this tendency is certainly not in line with the directives of the Council and of subsequent statements of the Magisterium. Difficulties both internal and external have weakened the Church's missionary thrust toward non-Christians, a fact which must arouse concern among all who believe in Christ. For in the Church's history, missionary drive has always been a sign of vitality, just as its lessening is a sign of a crisis of faith.[1]

Twenty-five years after the conclusion of the Council and the publication of the Decree on Missionary Activity *Ad Gentes,* fifteen years after the Apostolic Exhortation *Evangelii Nuntiandi* issued by Pope Paul VI, and in continuity with the magisterial teaching of my predecessors,[2] I wish to invite the

Church to *renew her missionary commitment.* The present document has as its goal an interior renewal of faith and Christian life. For missionary activity renews the Church, revitalizes faith and Christian identity, and offers fresh enthusiasm and new incentive. *Faith is strengthened when it is given to others!* It is in commitment to the Church's universal mission that the new evangelization of Christian peoples will find inspiration and support.

But what moves me even more strongly to proclaim the urgency of missionary evangelization is the fact that it is the primary service which the Church can render to every individual and to all humanity in the modern world, a world which has experienced marvelous achievements but which seems to have lost its sense of ultimate realities and of existence itself. "Christ the Redeemer," I wrote in my first encyclical, "fully reveals man to himself.... The person who wishes to understand himself thoroughly...must...draw near to Christ.... [The] Redemption that took place through the cross has definitively restored to man his dignity and given back meaning to his life in the world."[3]

I also have other reasons and aims: to respond to the many requests for a document of this kind; to clear up doubts and ambiguities regarding missionary activity *ad gentes,* and to confirm in their commitment those exemplary brothers and sisters dedicated to missionary activity and all those who assist them; to foster missionary vocations; to encourage theologians to explore and expound systematically the various aspects of missionary activity; to give a fresh impulse to missionary activity by fostering the commitment of the particular churches—especially those of recent origin—to send forth and receive missionaries; and to assure non-Christians and particularly the authorities of countries to which missionary activity is being directed that all of this has but one purpose: to serve man by revealing to him the love of God made manifest in Jesus Christ.

3. *Peoples everywhere, open the doors to Christ!* His Gospel in no way detracts from man's freedom, from the respect that is owed to every culture and to whatever is good in each religion. By accepting Christ, you open yourselves to the definitive Word of God, to the One in whom God has made himself fully known and has shown us the path to himself.

The number of those who do not know Christ and do not belong to the Church is constantly on the increase. Indeed, since the end of the Council it has almost doubled. When we consider this immense portion of humanity which is loved by the Father and for whom he sent his Son, the urgency of the Church's mission is obvious.

On the other hand, our own times offer the Church new opportunities in this field: we have witnessed the collapse of oppressive ideologies and political systems; the opening of frontiers and the formation of a more united world due to an increase in communications; the affirmation among peoples of the gospel values which Jesus made incarnate in his own life (peace, justice, brotherhood, concern for the needy); and a kind of soulless economic and technical development which only stimulates the search for the truth about God, about man and about the meaning of life itself.

God is opening before the Church the horizons of a humanity more fully prepared for the sowing of the Gospel. I sense that the moment has come to commit all of the Church's energies to a new evangelization and to the mission *ad gentes.* No believer in Christ, no institution of the Church can avoid this supreme duty: to proclaim Christ to all peoples.

Chapter I

Jesus Christ, the Only Savior

4. In my first encyclical, in which I set forth the program of my Pontificate, I said that "the Church's fundamental function in every age, and particularly in ours, is to direct man's gaze, to point the awareness and experience of the whole of humanity toward the mystery of Christ."[4]

The Church's universal mission is born of faith in Jesus Christ, as is stated in our Trinitarian profession of faith: "I believe in one Lord, Jesus Christ, the only Son of God, eternally begotten of the Father.... For us men and for our salvation he came down from heaven: by the power of the Holy Spirit he became incarnate from the Virgin Mary, and was made man."[5] The redemption event brings salvation to all, "for each one is included in the mystery of the redemption and with each one Christ has united himself forever through this mystery."[6] It is only in faith that the Church's mission can be understood and only in faith that it finds its basis.

Nevertheless, also as a result of the changes which have taken place in modern times and the spread of new theological ideas, some people wonder: *Is missionary work among non-Christians still relevant?* Has it not been replaced by inter-religious dialogue? Is not human development an adequate goal of the Church's mission? Does not respect for conscience and for freedom exclude all efforts at conversion?

Is it not possible to attain salvation in any religion? *Why then should there be missionary activity?*

"No one comes to the Father, but by me" (Jn 14:6)

5. If we go back to the beginnings of the Church, we find a clear affirmation that Christ is the one Savior of all, the only one able to reveal God and lead to God. In reply to the Jewish religious authorities who question the apostles about the healing of the lame man, Peter says: "By the name of Jesus Christ of Nazareth whom you crucified, whom God raised from the dead, by him this man is standing before you well.... And there is salvation in no one else, for there is no other name under heaven given among men by which we must be saved" (Acts 4:10, 12). This statement, which was made to the Sanhedrin, has a universal value, since for all people—Jews and Gentiles alike—salvation can only come from Jesus Christ.

The universality of this salvation in Christ is asserted throughout the New Testament. St. Paul acknowledges the risen Christ as the Lord. He writes: "Although there may be so-called gods in heaven or on earth—as indeed there are many 'gods' and many 'lords'—yet for us there is one God, the Father, from whom are all things and for whom we exist, and one Lord, Jesus Christ, through whom are all things and through whom we exist" (1 Cor 8:5-6). One God and one Lord are asserted by way of contrast to the multitude of "gods" and "lords" commonly accepted. Paul reacts against the polytheism of the religious environment of his time and emphasizes what is characteristic of the Christian faith: belief in one God and in one Lord sent by God.

In the Gospel of St. John, this salvific universality of Christ embraces all the aspects of his mission of grace, truth and revelation: the Word is "the true light that enlightens every man" (Jn 1:9). And again, "no one has ever seen God; the only Son, who is in the bosom of the Father, he has made him known" (Jn 1:18; cf. Mt 11:27). God's revelation becomes definitive and complete through his only-begotten Son: "In many and various ways God spoke of old to our fathers by the prophets; but in these last days he has spoken to us by a Son, whom he appointed the heir of all things, through whom he also created the world" (Heb 1:1-2; cf. Jn 14:6). In this definitive Word of his revelation, God has made himself known in the fullest possible way. He has revealed to mankind *who he is.* This definitive self-revelation of God is the fundamental reason why the Church is missionary by her very nature. She cannot do other than proclaim the Gospel, that is, the fullness of the truth which God has enabled us to know about himself.

Christ is the one mediator between God and mankind: "For there is one God, and there is one mediator between God and men, the man Christ Jesus, who gave himself as a ransom for all, the testimony to which was borne at the proper time. For this I was appointed a preacher and apostle (I am telling the truth, I am not lying), a teacher of the Gentiles in faith and truth" (1 Tm 2:5-7; cf. Heb 4:14-16). No one, therefore, can enter into communion with God except through Christ, by the working of the Holy Spirit. Christ's one, universal mediation, far from being an obstacle on the journey toward God, is the way established by God himself, a fact of which Christ is fully aware. Although participated forms of mediation of different kinds and degrees are not excluded, they acquire meaning and value *only* from Christ's own mediation, and they cannot be understood as parallel or complementary to his.

6. To introduce any sort of separation between the Word and Jesus Christ is contrary to the Christian faith. St. John

clearly states that the Word, who "was in the beginning with God," is the very one who "became flesh" (Jn 1:2, 14). Jesus is the Incarnate Word—a single and indivisible person. One cannot separate Jesus from the Christ or speak of a "Jesus of history" who would differ from the "Christ of faith." The Church acknowledges and confesses Jesus as "the Christ, the Son of the living God" (Mt 16:16): Christ is none other than Jesus of Nazareth; he is the Word of God made man for the salvation of all. In Christ "the whole fullness of deity dwells bodily" (Col 2:9) and "from his fullness have we all received" (Jn 1:16). The "only Son, who is in the bosom of the Father" (Jn 1:18) is "the beloved Son, in whom we have redemption.... For in him all the fullness of God was pleased to dwell, and through him to reconcile to himself all things, whether on earth or in heaven, making peace by the blood of his Cross" (Col 1:13-14, 19-20). It is precisely this uniqueness of Christ which gives him an absolute and universal significance, whereby, while belonging to history, he remains history's center and goal:[7] "I am the Alpha and the Omega, the first and the last, the beginning and the end" (Rv 22:13).

Thus, although it is legitimate and helpful to consider the various aspects of the mystery of Christ, we must never lose sight of its unity. In the process of discovering and appreciating the manifold gifts—especially the spiritual treasures—that God has bestowed on every people, we cannot separate those gifts from Jesus Christ, who is at the center of God's plan of salvation. Just as "by his incarnation the Son of God united himself in some sense with every human being," so too "we are obliged to hold that the Holy Spirit offers everyone the possibility of sharing in the Paschal Mystery in a manner known to God."[8] God's plan is "to unite all things in Christ, things in heaven and things on earth" (Eph 1:10).

Faith in Christ Is Directed to Man's Freedom

7. The urgency of missionary activity derives from the *radical newness of life* brought by Christ and lived by his followers. This new life is a gift from God, and people are asked to accept and develop it, if they wish to realize the fullness of their vocation in conformity to Christ. The whole New Testament is a hymn to the new life of those who believe in Christ and live in his Church. Salvation in Christ, as witnessed to and proclaimed by the Church, is God's self-communication: "It is love which not only creates the good, but also grants participation in the very life of God: Father, Son and Holy Spirit. For he who loves desires to give himself."[9]

God offers mankind this newness of life. "Can one reject Christ and everything that he has brought about in the history of mankind? Of course one can. Man is free. He can say 'no' to God. He can say 'no' to Christ. But the fundamental question remains: Is it legitimate to do this? And what would make it legitimate?"[10]

8. In the modern world there is a tendency to reduce man to his horizontal dimension alone. But without an openness to the Absolute, what does man become? The answer to this question is found in the experience of every individual, but it is also written in the history of humanity with the blood shed in the name of ideologies or bypolitical regimes which have sought to build a "new humanity" without God.[11]

Moreover, the Second Vatican Council replies to those concerned with safeguarding freedom of conscience: "The human person has a right to religious freedom.... All should have such immunity from coercion by individuals, or by groups, or by any human power, that no one should be forced to act against his conscience in religious matters, nor prevented from acting according to his conscience, whether in private or in public, whether alone or in association with others, within due limits."[12]

Proclaiming Christ and bearing witness to him, when done in a way that respects consciences, does not violate freedom. Faith demands a free adherence on the part of man, but at the same time faith must also be offered to him, because the "multitudes have the right to know the riches of the mystery of Christ—riches in which we believe that the whole of humanity can find, in unsuspected fullness, everything that it is gropingly searching for concerning God, man and his destiny, life and death, and truth.... This is why the Church keeps her missionary spirit alive, and even wishes to intensify it in the moment of history in which we are living."[13] But it must also be stated, again with the Council, that "in accordance with their dignity as persons, equipped with reason and free will and endowed with personal responsibility, all are impelled by their own nature and are bound by a moral obligation to seek truth, above all religious truth. They are further bound to hold to the truth once it is known, and to regulate their whole lives by its demands."[14]

The Church As Sign and Instrument of Salvation

9. The first beneficiary of salvation is the Church. Christ won the Church for himself at the price of his own blood and made the Church his co-worker in the salvation of the world. Indeed, Christ dwells within the Church. She is his Bride. It is he who causes her to grow. He carries out his mission through her.

The Council makes frequent reference to the Church's role in the salvation of mankind. While acknowledging that God loves all people and grants them the possibility of being saved (cf. 1 Tm 2:4),[15] the Church believes that God has established Christ as the one mediator and that she herself has been established as the universal sacrament of salvation.[16] "To this catholic unity of the people of God, therefore,...all are called, and they belong to it or are ordered to it in various ways, whether they be Catholic faithful or others who believe in Christ or finally all people everywhere who by the grace of God are called to salvation."[17] It is necessary to keep these two truths together, namely, the real possibility of salvation in Christ for all mankind and the necessity of the Church for salvation. Both these truths help us to understand the *one mystery of salvation,* so that we can come to know God's mercy and our own responsibility. Salvation, which always remains a gift of the Holy Spirit, requires man's cooperation, both to save himself and to save others. This is God's will, and this is why he established the Church and made her a part of his plan of salvation. Referring to "this messianic people," the Council says: "It has been set up by Christ as a communion of life, love and truth; by him too it is taken up as the instrument of salvation for all, and sent on a mission to the whole world as the light of the world and the salt of the earth."[18]

Salvation in Christ Is Offered to All

10. The universality of salvation means that it is granted not only to those who explicitly believe in Christ and have entered the Church. Since salvation is offered to all, it must be made concretely available to all. But it is clear that today, as in the past, many people do not have an opportunity to come to know or accept the gospel revelation or to enter the Church. The social and cultural conditions in which they live do not permit this, and frequently they have been brought up in other religious traditions. For such people salvation in Christ is accessible by virtue of a grace which, while having a mysterious

relationship to the Church, does not make them formally part of the Church but enlightens them in a way which is accommodated to their spiritual and material situation. This grace comes from Christ; it is the result of his Sacrifice and is communicated by the Holy Spirit. It enables each person to attain salvation through his or her free cooperation.

For this reason the Council, after affirming the centrality of the Paschal Mystery, went on to declare that "this applies not only to Christians but to all people of good will in whose hearts grace is secretly at work. Since Christ died for everyone, and since the ultimate calling of each of us comes from God and is therefore a universal one, we are obliged to hold that the Holy Spirit offers everyone the possibility of sharing in this Paschal Mystery in a manner known to God."[19]

"We cannot but speak" (Acts 4:20)

11. What then should be said of the objections already mentioned regarding the mission *ad gentes?* While respecting the beliefs and sensitivities of all, we must first clearly affirm our faith in Christ, the one Savior of mankind, a faith we have received as a gift from on high, not as a result of any merit of our own. We say with Paul, "I am not ashamed of the Gospel: it is the power of God for salvation to everyone who has faith" (Rom 1:16). Christian martyrs of all times—including our own—have given and continue to give their lives in order to bear witness to this faith, in the conviction that every human being needs Jesus Christ, who has conquered sin and death and reconciled mankind to God.

Confirming his words by miracles and by his resurrection from the dead, Christ proclaimed himself to be the Son of God dwelling in intimate union with the Father, and was recognized as such by his disciples. The Church offers mankind the

Gospel, that prophetic message which responds to the needs and aspirations of the human heart and always remains "Good News." The Church cannot fail to proclaim that Jesus came to reveal the face of God and to merit salvation for all humanity by his cross and resurrection.

To the question, *"why mission?"* we reply with the Church's faith and experience that true liberation consists in opening oneself to the love of Christ. In him, and only in him, are we set free from all alienation and doubt, from slavery to the power of sin and death. Christ is truly "our peace" (Eph 2:14); "the love of Christ impels us" (2 Cor 5:14), giving meaning and joy to our life. *Mission is an issue of faith,* an accurate indicator of our faith in Christ and his love for us.

The temptation today is to reduce Christianity to merely human wisdom, a pseudo-science of well-being. In our heavily secularized world a "gradual secularization of salvation" has taken place, so that people strive for the good of man, but man who is truncated, reduced to his merely horizontal dimension. We know, however, that Jesus came to bring integral salvation, one which embraces the whole person and all mankind, and opens up the wondrous prospect of divine filiation. *Why mission?* Because to us, as to St. Paul, "this grace was given, to preach to the Gentiles the unsearchable riches of Christ" (Eph 3:8). Newness of life in him is the "Good News" for men and women of every age: all are called to it and destined for it. Indeed, all people are searching for it, albeit at times in a confused way, and have a right to know the value of this gift and to approach it freely. The Church, and every individual Christian within her, may not keep hidden or monopolize this newness and richness which has been received from God's bounty in order to be communicated to all mankind.

This is why the Church's mission derives not only from the Lord's mandate but also from the profound demands of

God's life within us. Those who are incorporated in the Catholic Church ought to sense their privilege and for that very reason their greater obligation of *bearing witness to the faith and to the Christian life* as a service to their brothers and sisters and as a fitting response to God. They should be ever mindful that "they owe their distinguished status not to their own merits but to Christ's special grace; and if they fail to respond to this grace in thought, word and deed, not only will they not be saved, they will be judged more severely."[20]

Chapter II

The Kingdom of God

12. "It is 'God, who is rich in mercy' whom Jesus Christ has revealed to us as Father: it is his very Son who, in himself, has manifested him and made him known to us."[21] I wrote this at the beginning of my Encyclical *Dives in Misericordia,* to show that Christ is the revelation and incarnation of the Father's mercy. Salvation consists in believing and accepting the mystery of the Father and of his love, made manifest and freely given in Jesus through the Spirit. In this way the kingdom of God comes to be fulfilled: the kingdom prepared for in the Old Testament, brought about by Christ and in Christ, and proclaimed to all peoples by the Church, which works and prays for its perfect and definitive realization.

The Old Testament attests that God chose and formed a people for himself, in order to reveal and carry out his loving plan. But at the same time God is the Creator and Father of all people; he cares and provides for them, extending his blessing to all (cf. Gn 12:3); he has established a covenant with all of them (cf. Gn 9:1-17). Israel experiences a personal and saving God (cf. Dt 4:37; 7:6-8; Is 43:1-7) and becomes his witness and interpreter among the nations. In the course of her history, Israel comes to realize that her election has a universal meaning (cf. for example Is 2:2-5; 25:6-8; 60:1-6; Jer 3:17; 16:19).

Christ Makes the Kingdom Present

13. Jesus of Nazareth brings God's plan to fulfillment. After receiving the Holy Spirit at his Baptism, Jesus makes clear his messianic calling: he goes about Galilee "preaching the Gospel of God and saying: 'The time is fulfilled, and the kingdom of God is at hand; repent and believe in the Gospel'" (Mk 1:14-15; cf. Mt 4:17; Lk 4:43). The proclamation and establishment of God's kingdom are the purpose of his mission: "I was sent for this purpose" (Lk 4:43). But that is not all. Jesus himself is the "Good News," as he declares at the very beginning of his mission in the synagogue at Nazareth, when he applies to himself the words of Isaiah about the Anointed One sent by the Spirit of the Lord (cf. Lk 4:14-21). Since the "Good News" is Christ, there is an identity between the message and the messenger, between saying, doing and being. His power, the secret of the effectiveness of his actions, lies in his total identification with the message he announces: he proclaims the "Good News" not just by what he says or does, but by what he is.

The ministry of Jesus is described in the context of his journeys within his homeland. Before Easter, the scope of his mission was focused on Israel. Nevertheless, Jesus offers a new element of extreme importance. The eschatological reality is not relegated to a remote "end of the world," but is already close and at work in our midst. The kingdom of God is at hand (cf. Mk 1:15); its coming is to be prayed for (cf. Mt 6:10); faith can glimpse it already at work in signs such as miracles (cf. Mt 11:4-5) and exorcisms (cf. Mt 12:25-28), in the choosing of the Twelve (cf. Mk 3:13-19), and in the proclamation of the Good News to the poor (cf. Lk 4:18). Jesus' encounters with Gentiles make it clear that entry into the kingdom comes through faith and conversion (cf. Mk 1:15), and not merely by reason of ethnic background.

The kingdom which Jesus inaugurates is the kingdom of God. Jesus himself reveals who this God is, the One whom he addresses by the intimate term "Abba," Father (cf. Mk 14:36). God, as revealed above all in the parables (cf. Lk 15:3-32; Mt 20:1-16), is sensitive to the needs and sufferings of every human being: he is a Father filled with love and compassion, who grants forgiveness and freely bestows the favors asked of him.

St. John tells us that "God is love" (1 Jn 4:8, 16). Every person therefore is invited to "repent" and to "believe" in God's merciful love. The kingdom will grow insofar as every person learns to turn to God in the intimacy of prayer as to a Father (cf. Lk 11:2; Mt 23:9) and strives to do his will (cf. Mt 7:21).

Characteristics of the Kingdom and Its Demands

14. Jesus gradually reveals the characteristics and demands of the kingdom through his words, his actions and his own person.

The kingdom of God is meant for all mankind, and all people are called to become members of it. To emphasize this fact, Jesus drew especially near to those on the margins of society, and showed them special favor in announcing the Good News. At the beginning of his ministry he proclaimed that he was "anointed...to preach good news to the poor" (Lk 4:18). To all who are victims of rejection and contempt Jesus declares: "Blessed are you poor" (Lk 6:20). What is more, he enables such individuals to experience liberation even now, by being close to them, going to eat in their homes (cf. Lk 5:30; 15:2), treating them as equals and friends (cf. Lk 7:34), and making them feel loved by God, thus revealing his tender care for the needy and for sinners (cf. Lk 15:1-32).

The liberation and salvation brought by the kingdom of God come to the human person both in his physical and spiritual dimensions. Two gestures are characteristic of Jesus' mission: healing and forgiving. Jesus' many healings clearly show his great compassion in the face of human distress, but they also signify that in the kingdom there will no longer be sickness or suffering, and that his mission, from the very beginning, is meant to free people from these evils. In Jesus' eyes, healings are also a sign of spiritual salvation, namely liberation from sin. By performing acts of healing, he invites people to faith, conversion and the desire for forgiveness (cf. Lk 5:24). Once there is faith, healing is an encouragement to go further: it leads to salvation (cf. Lk 18:42-43). The acts of liberation from demonic possession—the supreme evil and symbol of sin and rebellion against God—are signs that indeed "the kingdom of God has come upon you" (Mt 12:28).

15. The kingdom aims at transforming human relationships; it grows gradually as people slowly learn to love, forgive and serve one another. Jesus sums up the whole Law, focusing it on the commandment of love (cf. Mt 22:34-40; Lk 10:25-28). Before leaving his disciples, he gives them a "new commandment": "Love one another; even as I have loved you" (Jn 13:34; cf. 15:12). Jesus' love for the world finds its highest expression in the gift of his life for mankind (cf. Jn 15:13), which manifests the love which the Father has for the world (cf. Jn 3:16). The kingdom's nature, therefore, is one of communion among all human beings—with one another and with God.

The kingdom is the concern of everyone: individuals, society, and the world. Working for the kingdom means acknowledging and promoting God's activity, which is present in human history and transforms it. Building the kingdom means working for liberation from evil in all its forms. In a word, the kingdom of God is the manifestation and the realization of God's plan of salvation in all its fullness.

In the Risen Christ God's Kingdom Is Fulfilled and Proclaimed

16. By raising Jesus from the dead, God has conquered death, and in Jesus he has definitely inaugurated his kingdom. During his earthly life, Jesus was the Prophet of the kingdom; after his passion, resurrection and ascension into heaven he shares in God's power and in his dominion over the world (cf. Mt 28:18; Acts 2:36; Eph 1:18-21). The resurrection gives a universal scope to Christ's message, his actions and whole mission. The disciples recognize that the kingdom is already present in the person of Jesus and is slowly being established within man and the world through a mysterious connection with him.

Indeed, after the resurrection, the disciples preach the kingdom by proclaiming Jesus crucified and risen from the dead. In Samaria, Philip "preached good news about the kingdom of God and the name of Jesus Christ" (Acts 8:12). In Rome, we find Paul "preaching the kingdom of God and teaching about the Lord Jesus Christ" (Acts 28:31). The first Christians also proclaim "the kingdom of Christ and of God" (Eph 5:5; cf. Rev 11:15; 12:10), or "the kingdom of our Lord and Savior Jesus Christ" (2 Pt 1:11). The preaching of the early Church was centered on the proclamation of Jesus Christ, with whom the kingdom was identified. Now, as then, there is a need to unite *the proclamation of the kingdom of God* (the content of Jesus' own "kerygma") and *the proclamation of the Christ-event* (the "kerygma" of the apostles). The two

27

proclamations are complementary; each throws light on the other.

The Kingdom in Relation to Christ and the Church

17. Nowadays the kingdom is much spoken of, but not always in a way consonant with the thinking of the Church. In fact, there are ideas about salvation and mission which can be called "anthropocentric" in the reductive sense of the word, inasmuch as they are focused on man's earthly needs. In this view, the kingdom tends to become something completely human and secularized; what counts are programs and struggles for a liberation which is socio-economic, political and even cultural, but within a horizon that is closed to the transcendent. Without denying that on this level too there are values to be promoted, such a notion nevertheless remains within the confines of a kingdom of man, deprived of its authentic and profound dimensions. Such a view easily translates into one more ideology of purely earthly progress. The kingdom of God, however, "is not of this world...is not from the world" (Jn 18:36).

There are also conceptions which deliberately emphasize the kingdom and which describe themselves as "kingdom-centered." They stress the image of a Church which is not concerned about herself, but which is totally concerned with bearing witness to and serving the kingdom. It is a "Church for others" just as Christ is the "man for others." The Church's task is described as though it had to proceed in two directions: on the one hand promoting such "values of the kingdom" as peace, justice, freedom, brotherhood, etc., while on the other hand fostering dialogue between peoples, cultures and religions, so that through a mutual enrichment they might help the world to be renewed and to journey ever closer toward the kingdom.

Together with positive aspects, these conceptions often reveal negative aspects as well. First, they are silent about Christ: the kingdom of which they speak is "theocentrically" based, since, according to them, Christ cannot be understood by those who lack Christian faith, whereas different peoples, cultures and religions are capable of finding common ground in the one divine reality, by whatever name it is called. For the same reason they put great stress on the mystery of creation, which is reflected in the diversity of cultures and beliefs, but they keep silent about the mystery of redemption. Furthermore, the kingdom, as they understand it, ends up either leaving very little room for the Church or undervaluing the Church in reaction to a presumed "ecclesiocentrism" of the past, and because they consider the Church herself only a sign, for that matter a sign not without ambiguity.

18. This is not the kingdom of God as we know it from Revelation. The kingdom cannot be detached either from Christ or from the Church.

As has already been said, Christ not only proclaimed the kingdom, but in him the kingdom itself became present and was fulfilled. This happened not only through his words and his deeds: "Above all,...the kingdom is made manifest in the very person of Christ, Son of God and Son of Man, who came 'to serve and to give his life as a ransom for many' (Mk 10:45)."[22] The kingdom of God is not a concept, a doctrine, or a program subject to free interpretation, but it is before all else *a person* with the face and name of Jesus of Nazareth, the image of the invisible God.[23] If the kingdom is separated from Jesus, it is no longer the kingdom of God which he revealed. The result is a distortion of the meaning of the kingdom, which runs the risk of being transformed into a purely human or ideological goal, and a distortion of the identity of Christ, who no longer appears as the Lord to whom everything must one day be subjected (cf. 1 Cor 15:27).

Likewise, one may not separate the kingdom from the Church. It is true that the Church is not an end unto herself, since she is ordered toward the kingdom of God of which she is the seed, sign and instrument. Yet, while remaining distinct from Christ and the kingdom, the Church is indissolubly united to both. Christ endowed the Church, his body, with the fullness of the benefits and means of salvation. The Holy Spirit dwells in her, enlivens her with his gifts and charisms, sanctifies, guides and constantly renews her.[24] The result is a unique and special relationship which, while not excluding the action of Christ and the Spirit outside the Church's visible boundaries, confers upon her a specific and necessary role; hence the Church's special connection with the kingdom of God and of Christ, which she has "the mission of announcing and inaugurating among all peoples."[25]

19. It is within this overall perspective that the reality of the kingdom is understood. Certainly, the kingdom demands the promotion of human values, as well as those which can properly be called "evangelical," since they are intimately bound up with the "Good News." But this sort of promotion, which is at the heart of the Church, must not be detached from or opposed to other fundamental tasks, such as proclaiming Christ and his Gospel, and establishing and building up communities which make present and active within mankind the living image of the kingdom. One need not fear falling thereby into a form of "ecclesiocentrism." Pope Paul VI, who affirmed the existence of "a profound link between Christ, the Church and evangelization,"[26] also said that the Church "is not an end unto herself, but rather is fervently concerned to be completely of Christ, in Christ and for Christ, as well as completely of men, among men and for men."[27]

The Church at the Service of the Kingdom

20. The Church is effectively and concretely at the service of the kingdom. This is seen especially in her preaching, which is a call to conversion. Preaching constitutes the Church's first and fundamental way of serving the coming of the kingdom in individuals and in human society. Eschatological salvation begins even now in newness of life in Christ: "To all who believed in him, who believed in his name, he gave power to become children of God" (Jn 1:12).

The Church, then, serves the kingdom by establishing communities and founding new particular churches, and by guiding them to mature faith and charity in openness toward others, in service to individuals and society, and in understanding and esteem for human institutions.

The Church serves the kingdom by spreading throughout the world the "gospel values" which are an expression of the kingdom and which help people to accept God's plan. It is true that the inchoate reality of the kingdom can also be found beyond the confines of the Church among peoples everywhere, to the extent that they live "gospel values" and are open to the working of the Spirit who breathes when and where he wills (cf. Jn 3:8). But it must immediately be added that this temporal dimension of the kingdom remains incomplete unless it is related to the kingdom of Christ present in the Church and straining towards eschatological fullness.[28]

The many dimensions of the kingdom of God[29] do not weaken the foundations and purposes of missionary activity, but rather strengthen and extend them. The Church is the sacrament of salvation for all mankind, and her activity is not limited only to those who accept her message. She is a dynamic force in mankind's journey toward the eschatological kingdom, and is the sign and promoter of gospel values.[30]

The Church contributes to mankind's pilgrimage of conversion to God's plan through her witness and through such activities as dialogue, human promotion, commitment to justice and peace, education and the care of the sick, and aid to the poor and to children. In carrying on these activities, however, she never loses sight of the priority of the transcendent and spiritual realities which are premises of eschatological salvation.

Finally, the Church serves the kingdom by her intercession, since the kingdom by its very nature is God's gift and work, as we are reminded by the gospel parables and by the prayer which Jesus taught us. We must ask for the kingdom, welcome it and make it grow within us; but we must also work together so that it will be welcomed and will grow among all people, until the time when Christ "delivers the kingdom to God the Father" and "God will be everything to everyone" (cf. 1 Cor 15:24, 28).

Chapter III

The Holy Spirit:
The Principal Agent of Mission

21. "At the climax of Jesus' messianic mission, the Holy Spirit becomes present in the Paschal Mystery in all of his divine subjectivity: as the one who is now to continue the salvific work rooted in the sacrifice of the cross. Of course Jesus entrusts this work to human beings: to the apostles, to the Church. Nevertheless, in and through them the Holy Spirit remains the transcendent and principal agent for the accomplishment of this work in the human spirit and in the history of the world."[31]

The Holy Spirit is indeed the principal agent of the whole of the Church's mission. His action is preeminent in the mission *ad gentes,* as can clearly be seen in the early Church: in the conversion of Cornelius (cf. Acts 10), in the decisions made about emerging problems (cf. Acts 15) and in the choice of regions and peoples to be evangelized (cf. Acts 16:6ff). The Spirit worked through the apostles, but at the same time he was also at work in those who heard them: "Through his action the Good News takes shape in human minds and hearts and extends through history. In all of this it is the Holy Spirit who gives life."[32]

Sent Forth "to the end of the earth" (Acts 1:8)

22. All the Evangelists, when they describe the risen Christ's meeting with his apostles, conclude with the "missionary mandate": "All authority in heaven and on earth has been given to me. Go therefore and make disciples of all nations,...and lo, I am with you always, to the close of the age" (Mt 28:18-20; cf. Mk 16:15-18; Lk 24:46-49; Jn 20:21-23).

This is *a sending forth in the Spirit,* as is clearly apparent in the Gospel of John: Christ sends his own into the world, just as the Father has sent him, and to this end he gives them the Spirit. Luke, for his part, closely links the witness the apostles are to give to Christ with the working of the Spirit, who will enable them to fulfill the mandate they have received.

23. The different versions of the "missionary mandate" contain common elements as well as characteristics proper to each. Two elements, however, are found in all the versions. First, there is the universal dimension of the task entrusted to the apostles, who are sent to "all nations" (Mt 28:19); "into all the world and...to the whole creation" (Mk 16:15); to "all nations" (Lk 24:47); "to the end of the earth" (Acts 1:8). Secondly, there is the assurance given to the apostles by the Lord that they will not be alone in the task, but will receive the strength and the means necessary to carry out their mission. The reference here is to the presence and power of the Spirit and the help of Jesus himself: "And they went forth and preached everywhere, while the Lord worked with them" (Mk 16:20).

As for the different emphases found in each version, Mark presents mission as proclamation or kerygma: "Preach the Gospel" (Mk 16:15). His aim is to lead his readers to repeat Peter's profession of faith: "You are the Christ" (Mk 8:29), and to say with the Roman centurion who stood before the body of Jesus on the cross: "Truly this man was the Son of God!" (Mk 15:39) In Matthew, the missionary emphasis is placed on the foundation of the Church and on her teaching (cf. Mt 28:19-20; 16:18). According to him, the mandate shows that the proclamation of the Gospel must be completed by a specific ecclesial and sacramental catechesis. In Luke, mission is presented as witness (cf. Lk 24:48; Acts 1:8), centered especially on the resurrection (cf. Acts 1:22). The missionary is invited to believe in the transforming power of the Gospel and to proclaim what Luke presents so well, that is, conversion to God's love and mercy, the experience of a complete liberation which goes to the root of all evil, namely sin.

John is the only Evangelist to speak explicitly of a "mandate," a word equivalent to "mission." He directly links the mission which Jesus entrusts to his disciples with the mission which he himself has received from the Father: "As the Father has sent me, even so I send you" (Jn 20:21). Addressing the Father, Jesus says: "As you sent me into the world, so I have sent them into the world" (Jn 17:18). The entire missionary sense of John's Gospel is expressed in the "priestly prayer": "This is eternal life, that they know you the only true God, and Jesus Christ whom you have sent" (Jn 17:3). The ultimate purpose of mission is to enable people to share in the communion which exists between the Father and the Son. The disciples are to live in unity with one another, remaining in the Father and the Son, so that the world may know and believe (cf. Jn 17:21-23). This is a very important missionary text. It makes us understand that we are missionaries above all because of *what we are* as a Church whose innermost life is unity in love, even before we become missionaries *in word or deed.*

The four Gospels therefore bear witness to a certain pluralism within the fundamental unity of the same mission, a pluralism which reflects different experiences and situations within the first Christian communities. It is also the result of the driving force of the Spirit himself; it encourages us to pay heed to the variety of missionary charisms and to the diversity of circumstances and peoples. Nevertheless, all the Evangelists stress that the mission of the disciples is to cooperate in the mission of Christ: "Lo, I am with you always, to the close of the age" (Mt 28:20). Mission, then, is based not on human abilities but on the power of the risen Lord.

The Spirit Directs the Church's Mission

24. The mission of the Church, like that of Jesus, is God's work or, as Luke often puts it, the work of the Spirit. After the resurrection and ascension of Jesus, the apostles have a powerful experience which completely transforms them: the experience of Pentecost. The coming of the Holy Spirit makes them *witnesses* and *prophets* (cf. Acts 1:8; 2:17-18). It fills them with a serene courage which impels them to pass on to others their experience of Jesus and the hope which motivates them. The Spirit gives them the ability to bear witness to Jesus with "boldness."[33] When the first evangelizers go down from Jerusalem, the Spirit becomes even more of a "guide," helping them to choose both those to whom they are to go and the places to which their missionary journey is to take them. The working of the Spirit is manifested particularly in the impetus given to the mission which, in accordance with Christ's words, spreads out from Jerusalem to all of Judea and Samaria, and to the farthest ends of the earth.

The Acts of the Apostles records six summaries of the "missionary discourses" which were addressed to the Jews during the Church's infancy (cf. Acts 2:22-39; 3:12-26; 4:9-12; 5:29-32; 10:34-43; 13:16-41). These model speeches, delivered by Peter and by Paul, proclaim Jesus and invite those listening to "be converted," that is, to accept Jesus in faith and to let themselves be transformed in him by the Spirit.

Paul and Barnabas are impelled by the Spirit to go to the Gentiles (cf. Acts 13:46-48), a development not without certain tensions and problems. How are these converted Gentiles to live their faith in Jesus? Are they bound by the traditions of Judaism and the law of circumcision? At the first Council, which gathers the members of the different churches together with the apostles in Jerusalem, a decision is taken which is acknowledged as coming from the Spirit: it is not necessary for a Gentile to submit to the Jewish Law in order to become a Christian (cf. Acts 15:5-11, 28). From now on the Church opens her doors and becomes the house which all may enter, and in which all can feel at home, while keeping their own culture and traditions, provided that these are not contrary to the Gospel.

25. The missionaries continued along this path, taking into account people's hopes and expectations, their anguish and sufferings, as well as their culture, in order to proclaim to them salvation in Christ. The speeches in Lystra and Athens (cf. Acts 14:15-17; 17:22-31) are acknowledged as models for the evangelization of the Gentiles. In these speeches Paul enters into "dialogue" with the cultural and religious values of different peoples. To the Lycaonians, who practiced a cosmic religion, he speaks of religious experiences related to the cosmos. With the Greeks he discusses philosophy and quotes their own poets (cf. Acts 17:18, 26-28). The God whom Paul wishes to reveal is already present in their lives; indeed, this God has created them and mysteriously guides nations and history. But if they are to recognize the true God, they must abandon the false gods which they themselves have made and open themselves to the One whom God has sent to remedy

their ignorance and satisfy the longings of their hearts. These are speeches which offer an example of the inculturation of the Gospel.

Under the impulse of the Spirit, the Christian faith is decisively opened to the "nations." Witness to Christ spreads to the most important centers of the eastern Mediterranean and then to Rome and the far regions of the West. It is the Spirit who is the source of the drive to press on, not only geographically but also beyond the frontiers of race and religion, for a truly universal mission.

The Holy Spirit Makes the Whole Church Missionary

26. The Spirit leads the company of believers to "form a community," to be the Church. After Peter's first proclamation on the day of Pentecost and the conversions that followed, the first community takes shape (cf. Acts 2:42-47; 4:32-35).

One of the central purposes of mission is to bring people together in hearing the Gospel, in fraternal communion, in prayer and in the Eucharist. To live in "fraternal communion" (*koinonia*) means to be "of one heart and soul" (Acts 4:32), establishing fellowship from every point of view: human, spiritual and material. Indeed, a true Christian community is also committed to distributing earthly goods, so that no one is in want, and all can receive such goods "as they need" (cf. Acts 2:45; 4:35). The first communities, made up of "glad and generous hearts" (Acts 2:46), were open and missionary: they enjoyed "favor with all the people" (Acts 2:47). Even before activity, mission means witness and a way of life that shines out to others.[34]

27. The Acts of the Apostles indicates that the mission which was directed first to Israel and then to the Gentiles develops on many levels. First and foremost, there is the group of the Twelve which as a single body, led by Peter, proclaims

the Good News. Then there is the community of believers, which in its way of life and its activity bears witness to the Lord and converts the Gentiles (cf. Acts 2:46-47). Then there are the special envoys sent out to proclaim the Gospel. Thus the Christian community at Antioch sends its members forth on mission; having fasted, prayed and celebrated the Eucharist, the community recognizes that the Spirit has chosen Paul and Barnabas to be "sent forth" (cf. Acts 13:1-4). In its origins, then, mission is seen as a community commitment, a responsibility of the local church, which needs "missionaries" in order to push forward toward new frontiers. Side by side with those who had been sent forth, there were also others, who bore spontaneous witness to the newness which had transformed their lives, and who subsequently provided a link between the emerging communities and the Apostolic Church.

Reading the Acts of the Apostles helps us to realize that at the beginning of the Church the mission *ad gentes,* while it had missionaries dedicated "for life" by a special vocation, was in fact considered the normal outcome of Christian living, to which every believer was committed through the witness of personal conduct and through explicit proclamation whenever possible.

The Spirit Is Present and Active in Every Time and Place

28. The Spirit manifests himself in a special way in the Church and in her members. Nevertheless, his presence and activity are universal, limited neither by space nor time.[35] The Second Vatican Council recalls that the Spirit is at work in the heart of every person, through the "seeds of the Word," to be found in human initiatives—including religious ones—and in

man's efforts to attain truth, goodness and God himself.[36]

The Spirit offers the human race "the light and strength to respond to its highest calling"; through the Spirit, "mankind attains in faith to the contemplation and savoring of the mystery of God's design"; indeed, "we are obliged to hold that the Holy Spirit offers everyone the possibility of sharing in the Paschal Mystery in a manner known to God."[37] The Church "is aware that humanity is being continually stirred by the Spirit of God and can therefore never be completely indifferent to the problems of religion" and that "people will always...want to know what meaning to give their life, their activity and their death."[38] The Spirit, therefore, is at the very source of man's existential and religious questioning, a questioning which is occasioned not only by contingent situations but by the very structure of his being.[39]

The Spirit's presence and activity affect not only the individuals but also society and history, peoples, cultures and religions. Indeed, the Spirit is at the origin of the noble ideals and undertakings which benefit humanity on its journey through history: "The Spirit of God with marvelous foresight directs the course of the ages and renews the face of the earth."[40] The risen Christ "is now at work in human hearts through the strength of his Spirit, not only instilling a desire for the world to come but also thereby animating, purifying and reinforcing the noble aspirations which drive the human family to make its life one that is more human and to direct the whole earth to this end."[41] Again, it is the Spirit who sows the "seeds of the Word" present in various customs and cultures, preparing them for full maturity in Christ.[42]

29. Thus the Spirit, who "blows where he wills" (cf. Jn 3:8), who "was already at work in the world before Christ was glorified,"[43] and who "has filled the world,...holds all things

together [and] knows what is said" (Wis 1:7), leads us to broaden our vision in order to ponder his activity in every time and place.[44] I have repeatedly called this fact to mind, and it has guided me in my meetings with a wide variety of peoples. The Church's relationship with other religions is dictated by a twofold respect: "Respect for man in his quest for answers to the deepest questions of his life, and respect for the action of the Spirit in man."[45] Excluding any mistaken interpretation, the interreligious meeting held in Assisi was meant to confirm my conviction that "every authentic prayer is prompted by the Holy Spirit, who is mysteriously present in every human heart."[46]

This is the same Spirit who was at work in the Incarnation and in the life, death and resurrection of Jesus, and who is at work in the Church. He is therefore not an alternative to Christ, nor does he fill a sort of void which is sometimes suggested as existing between Christ and the Logos. Whatever the Spirit brings about in human hearts and in the history of peoples, in cultures and religions serves as a preparation for the Gospel[47] and can only be understood in reference to Christ, the Word who took flesh by the power of the Spirit "so that as perfectly human he would save all human beings and sum up all things."[48]

Moreover, the universal activity of the Spirit is not to be separated from his particular activity within the body of Christ, which is the Church. Indeed, it is always the Spirit who is at work, both when he gives life to the Church and impels her to proclaim Christ, and when he implants and develops his gifts in all individuals and peoples, guiding the Church to discover these gifts, to foster them and to receive them through dialogue. Every form of the Spirit's presence is to be welcomed with respect and gratitude, but the discernment of this presence is the responsibility of the Church, to which Christ gave his Spirit in order to guide her into all the truth (cf. Jn 16:13).

Missionary Activity Is Only Beginning

30. Our own time, with humanity on the move and in continual search, demands *a resurgence of the Church's missionary activity.* The horizons and possibilities for mission are growing ever wider, and we Christians are called to an apostolic courage based upon trust in the Spirit. *He is the principal agent of mission!*

The history of humanity has known many major turning points which have encouraged missionary outreach, and the Church, guided by the Spirit, has always responded to them with generosity and farsightedness. Results have not been lacking. Not long ago we celebrated the millennium of the evangelization of Rus' and the Slav peoples, and we are now preparing to celebrate the five hundredth anniversary of the evangelization of the Americas. Similarly, there have been recent commemorations of the centenaries of the first missions in various countries of Asia, Africa and Oceania. Today the Church must face other challenges and push forward to new frontiers, both in the initial mission *ad gentes* and in the new evangelization of those peoples who have already heard Christ proclaimed. Today all Christians, the particular churches and the universal Church, are called to have the same courage that inspired the missionaries of the past, and the same readiness to listen to the voice of the Spirit.

Chapter IV

The Vast Horizons of the Mission
Ad Gentes

31. The Lord Jesus sent his apostles to every person, people and place on earth. In the apostles, the Church received a universal mission—one which knows no boundaries—which involves the communication of salvation in its integrity according to that fullness of life which Christ came to bring (cf. Jn 10:10). The Church was "sent by Christ to reveal and communicate the love of God to all people and nations."[49]

This mission is one and undivided, having one origin and one final purpose; but within it, there are different tasks and kinds of activity. First, there is the missionary activity which we call *mission ad gentes,* in reference to the opening words of the Council's decree on this subject. This is one of the Church's fundamental activities: it is essential and never-ending. The Church, in fact, "cannot withdraw from her *permanent mission of bringing the Gospel* to the multitudes—the millions and millions of men and women—who as yet do not know Christ the Redeemer of humanity. In a specific way this is the missionary work which Jesus entrusted and still entrusts each day to his Church."[50]

A Complex and Ever Changing Religious Picture

32. Today we face a religious situation which is extremely

varied and changing. Peoples are on the move; social and religious realities which were once clear and well defined are today increasingly complex. We need only think of certain phenomena such as urbanization, mass migration, the flood of refugees, the de-christianization of countries with ancient Christian traditions, the increasing influence of the Gospel and its values in overwhelmingly non-Christian countries, and the proliferation of messianic cults and religious sects. Religious and social upheaval makes it difficult to apply in practice certain ecclesial distinctions and categories to which we have become accustomed. Even before the Council it was said that some Christian cities and countries had become "mission territories"; the situation has certainly not improved in the years since then.

On the other hand, missionary work has been very fruitful throughout the world, so that there are now well-established churches, sometimes so sound and mature that they are able to provide for the needs of their own communities and even send personnel to evangelize in other churches and territories. This is in contrast to some traditionally Christian areas which are in need of re-evangelization. As a result, some are questioning whether it is still appropriate to speak of *specific missionary activity* or specifically "missionary" areas, or whether we should speak instead of a *single missionary situation,* with one single mission, the same everywhere. The difficulty of relating this complex and changing reality to the mandate of evangelization is apparent in the "language of mission." For example, there is a certain hesitation to use the terms "mission" and "missionaries," which are considered obsolete and as having negative historical connotations. People prefer to use instead the noun "mission" in the singular and the adjective "missionary" to describe all the Church's activities.

This uneasiness denotes a real change, one which has certain positive aspects. The so-called return or "repatriation" of the *missions* into the Church's mission, the insertion of *missiology* into *ecclesiology,* and the integration of both areas into the Trinitarian plan of salvation, have given a fresh impetus to missionary activity itself, which is not considered a marginal task for the Church but is situated at the center of her life, as a fundamental commitment of the whole People of God. Nevertheless, care must be taken to avoid the risk of putting very different situations on the same level and of reducing, or even eliminating, the Church's mission and missionaries *ad gentes.* To say that the whole Church is missionary does not preclude the existence of a specific mission *ad gentes,* just as saying that all Catholics must be missionaries not only does not exclude, but actually requires that there be persons who have a specific vocation to be "life-long missionaries *ad gentes.*"

Mission Ad Gentes *Retains Its Value*

33. The fact that there is a diversity of activities *in the Church's one mission* is not intrinsic to that mission, but arises from the variety of circumstances in which that mission is carried out.[51] Looking at today's world from the viewpoint of evangelization, we can distinguish *three situations.*

First, there is the situation which the Church's missionary activity addresses: peoples, groups and socio-cultural contexts in which Christ and his Gospel are not known, or which lack Christian communities sufficiently mature to be able to incarnate the faith in their own environment and proclaim it to other groups. This is mission *ad gentes* in the proper sense of the term.[52]

Secondly, there are Christian communities with adequate and solid ecclesial structures. They are fervent in their faith and in Christian living. They bear witness to the Gospel in their surroundings and have a sense of commitment to the universal mission. In these communities the Church carries out her activity and pastoral care.

Thirdly, there is an intermediate situation, particularly in countries with ancient Christian roots, and occasionally in the younger Churches as well, where entire groups of the baptized have lost a living sense of the faith, or even no longer consider themselves members of the Church, and live a life far removed from Christ and his Gospel. In this case what is needed is a "new evangelization" or a "re-evangelization."

34. Missionary activity proper, namely the mission *ad gentes,* is directed to "peoples or groups who do not yet believe in Christ," "who are far from Christ," in whom the Church "has not yet taken root"[53] and whose culture has not yet been influenced by the Gospel.[54] It is distinct from other ecclesial activities inasmuch as it is addressed to groups and settings which are non-Christian because the preaching of the Gospel and the presence of the Church are either absent or insufficient. It can thus be characterized as the work of proclaiming Christ and his Gospel, building up the local Church and promoting the values of the kingdom. The specific nature of this mission *ad gentes* consists in its being addressed to "non-Christians." It is therefore necessary to ensure that this specifically "missionary work that Jesus entrusted and still entrusts each day to his Church"[55] does not become an indistinguishable part of the overall mission of the whole People of God and as a result become neglected or forgotten.

On the other hand, the boundaries between *pastoral care of the faithful, new evangelization* and *specific missionary activity* are not clearly definable, and it is unthinkable to create barriers between them or to put them into watertight compartments. Nevertheless, there must be no lessening of the impetus to preach the Gospel and to establish new churches among peoples or communities where they do not yet exist, for this is the first task of the Church, which has been sent forth to all peoples and to the very ends of the earth. Without the mission *ad gentes,* the Church's very missionary dimension would be deprived of its essential meaning and of the very activity that exemplifies it.

Also to be noted is the real and growing *interdependence* which exists between these various saving activities of the Church. Each of them influences, stimulates and assists the others. The missionary thrust fosters exchanges between the churches and directs them toward the larger world, with positive influences in every direction. The churches in traditionally Christian countries, for example, involved as they are in the challenging task of new evangelization, are coming to understand more clearly that they cannot be missionaries to non-Christians in other countries and continents unless they are seriously concerned about the non-Christians at home. Hence missionary activity *ad intra* is a credible sign and a stimulus for missionary activity *ad extra,* and vice versa.

To All Peoples, In Spite of Difficulties

35. The mission *ad gentes* faces an enormous task, which is in no way disappearing. Indeed, both from the numerical standpoint of demographic increase and from the socio-cultural standpoint of the appearance of new relationships, contacts and changing situations, the mission seems destined to have ever wider horizons. The task of proclaiming Jesus Christ to all peoples appears to be immense and out of all proportion to the Church's human resources.

The *difficulties* seem insurmountable and could easily lead to discouragement, if it were a question of a merely human enterprise. In certain countries missionaries are refused entry. In others, not only is evangelization forbidden but conversion as well, and even Christian worship. Elsewhere the obstacles are of a cultural nature: passing on the Gospel message seems irrelevant or incomprehensible, and conversion is seen as a rejection of one's own people and culture.

36. Nor are *difficulties* lacking *within* the People of God; indeed these difficulties are the most painful of all. As the first of these difficulties Pope Paul VI pointed to "the lack of fervor [which] is all the more serious because it comes from within. It is manifested in fatigue, disenchantment, compromise, lack of interest and above all lack of joy and hope."[56] Other great obstacles to the Church's missionary work include past and present divisions among Christians,[57] dechristianization within Christian countries, the decrease of vocations to the apostolate, and the counterwitness of believers and Christian communities failing to follow the model of Christ in their lives. But one of the most serious reasons for the lack of interest in the missionary task is a widespread indifferentism, which, sad to say, is found also among Christians. It is based on incorrect theological perspectives and is characterized by a religious relativism which leads to the belief that "one religion is as good as another." We can add, using the words of Pope Paul VI, that there are also certain "excuses which would impede evangelization. The most insidious of these excuses are certainly the ones which people claim to find support for in such and such a teaching of the Council."[58]

In this regard, I earnestly ask theologians and professional Christian journalists to intensify the service they render to the Church's mission in order to discover the deep meaning of their work, along the sure path of "thinking with the Church" *(sentire cum Ecclesia)*.

Internal and external difficulties must not make us pessimistic or inactive. What counts, here as in every area of Christian life, is the confidence that comes from faith, from the certainty that it is not we who are the principal agents of the Church's mission, but Jesus Christ and his Spirit. We are only co-workers, and when we have done all that we can, we must say: "We are unworthy servants; we have only done what was our duty" (Lk 17:10).

Parameters of the Church's Mission Ad Gentes

37. By virtue of Christ's universal mandate, the mission *ad gentes* knows no boundaries. Still, it is possible to determine certain parameters within which that mission is exercised, in order to gain a real grasp of the situation.

(a) *Territorial limits.* Missionary activity has normally been defined in terms of specific territories. The Second Vatican Council acknowledged the territorial dimension of the mission *ad gentes*,[59] a dimension which even today remains important for determining responsibilities, competencies and the geographical limits of missionary activity. Certainly, a universal mission implies a universal perspective. Indeed, the Church refuses to allow her missionary presence to be hindered by geographical boundaries or political barriers. But it is also true that missionary activity *ad gentes,* being different from the pastoral care of the faithful and the new evangelization of the non-practicing, is exercised within well-defined territories and groups of people.

The growth in the number of new churches in recent times should not deceive us. Within the territories entrusted to these churches—particularly in Asia, but also in Africa, Latin America and Oceania—there remain vast regions still to be evangelized. In many nations entire peoples and cultural areas of great importance have not yet been reached by the proclamation of the Gospel and the presence of the local church.[60] Even in traditionally Christian countries there are regions that are under the special structures of the mission *ad gentes,* with groups and areas not yet evangelized. Thus, in these countries too there is a need not only for a new evangelization, but also, in some cases, for an initial evangelization.[61]

Situations are not, however, the same everywhere. While acknowledging that statements about the missionary responsibility of the Church are not credible unless they are backed up by a serious commitment to a new evangelization in the traditionally Christian countries, it does not seem justified to regard as identical the situation of a people which has never known Jesus Christ and that of a people which has known him, accepted him and then rejected him, while continuing to live in a culture which in large part has absorbed gospel principles and values. These are two basically different situations with regard to the faith.

Thus the criterion of geography, although somewhat imprecise and always provisional, is still a valid indicator of the frontiers toward which missionary activity must be directed. There are countries and geographical and cultural areas which lack indigenous Christian communities. In other places, these communities are so small as not to be a clear sign of a Christian presence; or they lack the dynamism to evangelize their societies, or belong to a minority population not integrated into the dominant culture of the nation. Particularly in Asia, toward which the Church's mission *ad gentes* ought to be chiefly directed, Christians are a small minority, even though sometimes there are significant numbers of converts and outstanding examples of Christian presence.

(b) *New worlds and new social phenomena.* The rapid and profound transformations which characterize today's world, especially in the southern hemisphere, are having a powerful effect on the overall missionary picture. Where before there were stable human and social situations, today everything is in flux. One thinks, for example, of urbanization and the massive growth of cities, especially where demographic pressure is greatest. In not a few countries, over half the population already lives in a few "megalopolises," where human problems are often aggravated by the feeling of anonymity experienced by masses of people.

In the modern age, missionary activity has been carried out especially in isolated regions which are far from centers of civilization and which are hard to penetrate because of difficulties of communication, language or climate. Today the image of mission *ad gentes* is perhaps changing: efforts should be concentrated on the big cities, where new customs and styles of living arise together with new forms of culture and communication, which then influence the wider population. It is true that the "option for the neediest" means that we should not overlook the most abandoned and isolated human groups, but it is also true that individuals or small groups cannot be evangelized if we neglect the centers where a new humanity, so to speak, is emerging, and where new models of development are taking shape. The future of the younger nations is being shaped in the cities.

Speaking of the future, we cannot forget the young, who in many countries comprise more than half the population. How do we bring the message of Christ to non-Christian young people who represent the future of entire continents? Clearly, the ordinary means of pastoral work are not sufficient: what are needed are associations, institutions, special centers and groups, and cultural and social initiatives for young people. This is a field where modern ecclesial movements have ample room for involvement.

Among the great changes taking place in the contemporary world, migration has produced a new phenomenon: non-Christians are becoming very numerous in traditionally Christian countries, creating fresh opportunities for contacts and cultural exchanges, and calling the Church to hospitality, dialogue, assistance and, in a word, fraternity. Among migrants, refugees occupy a very special place and deserve the greatest attention. Today there are many millions of refugees in the world and their number is constantly increasing. They have fled from conditions of political oppression and inhuman misery, from famine and drought of catastrophic proportions. The Church must make them part of her overall apostolic concern.

Finally, we may mention the situations of poverty—often on an intolerable scale—which have been created in not a few countries, and which are often the cause of mass migration. The community of believers in Christ is challenged by these inhuman situations: the proclamation of Christ and the kingdom of God must become the means for restoring the human dignity of these people.

(c) *Cultural sectors: the modern equivalents of the Areopagus.* After preaching in a number of places, St. Paul arrived in Athens, where he went to the Areopagus and proclaimed the Gospel in language appropriate to and understandable in those surroundings (cf. Acts 17:22-31). At that time the Areopagus represented the cultural center of the learned people of Athens, and today it can be taken as a symbol of the new sectors in which the Gospel must be proclaimed.

The first Areopagus of the modern age is the *world of communications,* which is unifying humanity and turning it into what is known as a "global village." The means of social communication have become so important as to be for many the chief means of information and education, of guidance and inspiration in their behavior as individuals, families and within society at large. In particular, the younger generation is growing up in a world conditioned by the mass media. To some degree perhaps this Areopagus has been neglected. Generally, preference has been given to other means of preaching the Gospel and of Christian education, while the mass media are left to the initiative of individuals or small groups and enter into pastoral planning only in a secondary way. Involvement in the mass media, however, is not meant merely to strengthen the preaching of the Gospel. There is a deeper reality involved here: since the very evangelization of modern culture depends to a great extent on the influence of the media, it is not enough to use the media simply to spread the Christian message and the Church's authentic teaching. It is also necessary to integrate that message into the "new culture" created by modern communications. This is a complex issue, since the "new culture" originates not just from whatever content is eventually expressed, but from the very fact that there exist new ways of communicating, with new languages, new techniques and a new psychology. Pope Paul VI said that "the split between the Gospel and culture is undoubtedly the tragedy of our time,"[62] and the field of communications fully confirms this judgment.

There are many other forms of the "Areopagus" in the modern world toward which the Church's missionary activity ought to be directed; for example, commitment to peace, development and the liberation of peoples; the rights of individuals and peoples, especially those of minorities; the advancement of women and children; safeguarding the created world. These too are areas which need to be illuminated with the light of the Gospel.

We must also mention the immense "Areopagus" of culture, scientific research, and international relations which promote dialogue and open up new possibilities. We would do well to be attentive to these modern areas of activity and to be involved in them. People sense that they are, as it were, traveling together across life's sea, and that they are called to ever greater unity and solidarity. Solutions to pressing problems must be studied, discussed and worked out with the involvement of all. That is why international organizations and meetings are proving increasingly important in many sectors of human life, from culture to politics, from the economy to research. Christians who live and work in this international sphere must always remember their duty to bear witness to the Gospel.

38. Our times are both momentous and fascinating. While on the one hand people seem to be pursuing material prosperity and to be sinking ever deeper into consumerism and materialism, on the other hand we are witnessing a desperate search for meaning, the need for an inner life, and a desire to learn new forms and methods of meditation and prayer. Not only in cultures with strong religious elements, but also in secularized societies, the spiritual dimension of life is being sought after as an antidote to dehumanization. This phenomenon—the so-called "religious revival"—is not without ambiguity, but it also represents an opportunity. The Church has an immense spiritual patrimony to offer humankind, a heritage in Christ, who called himself "the way, and the truth, and the life" (Jn 14:6): it is the Christian path to meeting God, to prayer, to asceticism, and to the search for life's meaning. Here too there is an "Areopagus" to be evangelized.

Fidelity to Christ
and the Promotion of Human Freedom

39. All forms of missionary activity are marked by an awareness that one is furthering human freedom by proclaiming Jesus Christ. The Church must be faithful to Christ, whose

body she is, and whose mission she continues. She must necessarily "go the same road that Christ went—namely a road of poverty, obedience, service and self-sacrifice even unto death, from which he emerged a victor through his resurrection."[63] The Church is thus obliged to do everything possible to carry out her mission in the world and to reach all peoples. And she has the right to do this, a right given her by God for the accomplishment of his plan. Religious freedom, which is still at times limited or restricted, remains the premise and guarantee of all the freedoms that ensure the common good of individuals and peoples. It is to be hoped that authentic religious freedom will be granted to all people everywhere. The Church strives for this in all countries, especially in those with a Catholic majority, where she has greater influence. But it is not a question of the religion of the majority or the minority, but of an inalienable right of each and every human person.

On her part, the Church addresses people with full respect for their freedom.[64] Her mission does not restrict freedom but rather promotes it. *The Church proposes; she imposes nothing.* She respects individuals and cultures, and she honors the sanctuary of conscience. To those who for various reasons oppose missionary activity, the Church repeats: *Open the doors to Christ!*

Here I wish to address all the particular churches, both young and old. The world is steadily growing more united, and the gospel spirit must lead us to overcome cultural and nationalistic barriers, avoiding all isolationism. Pope Benedict XV already cautioned the missionaries of his time lest they "forget their proper dignity and think more of their earthly homeland than of their heavenly one."[65] This same advice is valid today for the particular churches: Open the doors to missionaries, for "each individual church that would voluntarily cut itself off from the universal Church would lose its relationship to God's plan and would be impoverished in its ecclesial mission."[66]

Directing Attention Toward the South and the East

40. Today missionary activity still represents the greatest challenge for the Church. As the end of the second millennium of the redemption draws near, it is clear that the peoples who have not yet received an initial proclamation of Christ constitute the majority of mankind. The results of missionary activity in modern times are certainly positive. The Church has been established on every continent; indeed today the majority of believers and particular churches is to be found no longer in Europe but on the continents which missionaries have opened up to the faith.

The fact remains however that the "ends of the earth" to which the Gospel must be brought are growing ever more distant. Tertullian's saying, that the Gospel has been proclaimed to all the earth and to all peoples,[67] is still very far from being a reality. The mission *ad gentes* is still in its infancy. New peoples appear on the world scene, and they too have a right to receive the proclamation of salvation. Population growth in non-Christian countries of the South and the East is constantly increasing the number of people who remain unaware of Christ's redemption.

We need therefore to direct our attention toward those geographical areas and cultural settings which still remain uninfluenced by the Gospel. All who believe in Christ should feel, as an integral part of their faith, an apostolic concern to pass on to others its light and joy. This concern must become, as it were, a hunger and thirst to make the Lord known, given the vastness of the non-Christian world.

Chapter V

The Paths of Mission

41. "Missionary activity is nothing other and nothing less than the manifestation or epiphany of God's plan and its fulfillment in the world and in history; in this history God, by means of missions, clearly accomplishes the history of salvation."[68] What paths does the Church follow in order to achieve this goal?

Mission is a single but complex reality, and it develops in a variety of ways. Among these ways, some have particular importance in the present situation of the Church and the world.

The First Form of Evangelization Is Witness

42. People today put more trust in witnesses than in teachers,[69] in experience than in teaching, and in life and action than in theories. The witness of a Christian life is the first and irreplaceable form of mission: Christ, whose mission we continue, is the "witness" *par excellence* (Rv 1:5; 3:14) and the model of all Christian witness. The Holy Spirit accompanies the Church along her way and associates her with the witness he gives to Christ (cf. Jn 15:26-27).

The first form of witness is *the very life of the missionary, of the Christian family,* and *of the ecclesial community,* which reveal a new way of living. The missionary who, despite all his or her human limitations and defects, lives a simple life, taking Christ as the model, is a sign of God and of transcendent realities. But everyone in the Church, striving to imitate the Divine Master, can and must bear this kind of witness;[70] in many cases it is the only possible way of being a missionary.

The evangelical witness which the world finds most appealing is that of concern for people, and of charity toward the poor, the weak and those who suffer. The complete generosity underlying this attitude and these actions stands in marked contrast to human selfishness. It raises precise questions which lead to God and to the Gospel. A commitment to peace, justice, human rights and human promotion is also a witness to the Gospel when it is a sign of concern for persons and is directed toward integral human development.[71]

43. Christians and Christian communities are very much a part of the life of their respective nations and can be a sign of the Gospel in their fidelity to their native land, people and national culture, while always preserving the freedom brought by Christ. Christianity is open to universal brotherhood, for all men and women are sons and daughters of the same Father and brothers and sisters in Christ.

The Church is called to bear witness to Christ by taking courageous and prophetic stands in the face of the corruption of political or economic power; by not seeking her own glory and material wealth; by using her resources to serve the poorest of the poor and by imitating Christ's own simplicity of life. The Church and her missionaries must also bear the witness of humility, above all with regard to themselves—a humility which allows them to make a personal and communal examination of conscience in order to correct in their behavior whatever is contrary to the Gospel and disfigures the face of Christ.

The Initial Proclamation of Christ the Savior

44. Proclamation is the permanent priority of mission. The Church cannot elude Christ's explicit mandate, nor deprive men and women of the "Good News" about their being loved and saved by God. "Evangelization will always contain—as the foundation, center and at the same time the summit of its dynamism—a clear proclamation that, in Jesus Christ...salvation is offered to all people, as a gift of God's grace and mercy."[72] All forms of missionary activity are directed to this proclamation, which reveals and gives access to the mystery hidden for ages and made known in Christ (cf. Eph 3:3-9; Col 1:25-29), the mystery which lies at the heart of the Church's mission and life, as the hinge on which all evangelization turns.

In the complex reality of mission, initial proclamation has a central and irreplaceable role, since it introduces man "into the mystery of the love of God, who invites him to enter into a personal relationship with himself in Christ"[73] and opens the way to conversion. Faith is born of preaching, and every ecclesial community draws its origin and life from the personal response of each believer to that preaching.[74] Just as the whole economy of salvation has its center in Christ, so too all missionary activity is directed to the proclamation of his mystery.

The subject of proclamation is Christ who was crucified, died and is risen: through him is accomplished our full and authentic liberation from evil, sin and death; through him God bestows "new life" that is divine and eternal. This is the "Good News" which changes man and his history, and which all peoples have a right to hear. This proclamation is to be made within the context of the lives of the individuals and peoples who receive it. It is to be made with an attitude of love and esteem toward those who hear it, in language which is practical and adapted to the situation. In this proclamation the Spirit is at work and establishes a communion between the missionary and his hearers, a communion which is possible inasmuch as both enter into communion with God the Father through Christ.[75]

45. Proclamation, because it is made in union with the entire ecclesial community, is never a merely personal act. The missionary is present and carries out his work by virtue of a mandate he has received; even if he finds himself alone, he remains joined by invisible but profound bonds to the evangelizing activity of the whole Church.[76] Sooner or later, his hearers come to recognize in him the community which sent him and which supports him.

Proclamation is inspired by faith, which gives rise to enthusiasm and fervor in the missionary. As already mentioned, the Acts of the Apostles uses the word *parrhesia* to describe this attitude, a word which means to speak frankly and with courage. This term is found also in St. Paul: "We had courage in our God to declare to you the Gospel of God in the face of great opposition" (1 Th 2:2); "Pray...also for me, that utterance may be given me in opening my mouth boldly to proclaim the mystery of the Gospel for which I am an ambassador in chains; that I may declare it boldly, as I ought to speak" (Eph 6:18-20).

In proclaiming Christ to non-Christians, the missionary is convinced that, through the working of the Spirit, there already exists in individuals and peoples an expectation, even if an unconscious one, of knowing the truth about God, about man, and about how we are to be set free from sin and death. The missionary's enthusiasm in proclaiming Christ comes from the conviction that he is responding to that expectation, and so he does not become discouraged or cease his witness even when he is called to manifest his faith in an environment that is hostile or indifferent. He knows that the Spirit of the Father is speaking through him (cf. Mt 10:17-20; Lk 12:11-12) and he can say with the apostles: "We are witnesses to these things, and so is the Holy Spirit" (Acts 5:32). He knows that he is not proclaiming a human truth, but the "word of God," which has an intrinsic and mysterious power of its own (cf. Rom 1:16).

The supreme test is the giving of one's life, to the point of accepting death in order to bear witness to one's faith in Jesus Christ. Throughout Christian history, martyrs, that is, "witnesses," have always been numerous and indispensable to the spread of the Gospel. In our own age, there are many: bishops, priests, men and women religious, lay people—often unknown heroes who give their lives to bear witness to the faith. They are *par excellence* the heralds and witnesses of the faith.

Conversion and Baptism

46. The proclamation of the Word of God has *Christian conversion* as its aim: a complete and sincere adherence to Christ and his Gospel through faith. Conversion is a gift of God, a work of the Blessed Trinity. It is the Spirit who opens people's hearts so that they can believe in Christ and "confess him" (cf. 1 Cor 12:3); of those who draw near to him through faith Jesus says: "No one can come to me unless the Father who sent me draws him" (Jn 6:44).

From the outset, conversion is expressed in faith which is total and radical, and which neither limits nor hinders God's gift. At the same time, it gives rise to a dynamic and lifelong process which demands a continual turning away from "life according to the flesh" to "life according to the Spirit" (cf. Rom 8:3-13). Conversion means accepting, by a personal decision, the saving sovereignty of Christ and becoming his disciple.

The Church calls all people to this conversion, following the example of John the Baptist, who prepared the way for Christ by "preaching a baptism of repentance for the forgiveness of sins" (Mk 1:4), as well as the example of Christ himself, who "after John was arrested,...came into Galilee preaching the Gospel of God and saying: 'The time is fulfilled, and the kingdom of God is at hand; *repent* and believe in the Gospel'" (Mk 1:14-15).

Nowadays the call to conversion which missionaries address to non-Christians is put into question or passed over in silence. It is seen as an act of "proselytizing"; it is claimed that it is enough to help people to become more human or more faithful to their own religion, that it is enough to build communities capable of working for justice, freedom, peace and solidarity. What is overlooked is that every person has the right to hear the "Good News" of the God who reveals and gives himself in Christ, so that each one can live out in its fullness his or her proper calling. This lofty reality is expressed in the words of Jesus to the Samaritan woman: "If you knew the gift of God," and in the unconscious but ardent desire of the woman: "Sir, give me this water, that I may not thirst" (Jn 4:10, 15).

47. The apostles, prompted by the Spirit, invited all to change their lives, to be converted and to be baptized. Immediately after the event of Pentecost, Peter spoke convincingly to the crowd: "When they heard this, they were cut to the heart, and said to Peter and the rest of the Apostles, 'Brethren, what shall we do?' And Peter said to them, *'Repent,* and be baptized every one of you in the name of Jesus Christ for the forgiveness of your sins; and you shall receive the gift of the Holy Spirit'" (Acts 2:37-38). That very day some three

thousand persons were baptized. And again, after the healing of the lame man, Peter spoke to the crowd and repeated: *"Repent* therefore, and turn again, that your sins may be blotted out!" (Acts 3:19)

Conversion to Christ is joined to Baptism not only because of the Church's practice, but also by the will of Christ himself, who sent the apostles to make disciples of all nations and to baptize them (cf. Mt 28:19). Conversion is also joined to Baptism because of the intrinsic need to receive the fullness of new life in Christ. As Jesus says to Nicodemus: "Truly, truly, I say to you, unless one is born of water and the Spirit, he cannot enter the kingdom of God" (Jn 3:5). In Baptism, in fact, we are born anew to the life of God's children, united to Jesus Christ and anointed in the Holy Spirit. Baptism is not simply a seal of conversion, and a kind of external sign indicating conversion and attesting to it. Rather, it is the sacrament which signifies and effects rebirth from the Spirit, establishes real and unbreakable bonds with the Blessed Trinity, and makes us members of the Body of Christ, which is the Church.

All this needs to be said, since not a few people, precisely in those areas involved in the mission *ad gentes,* tend to separate conversion to Christ from Baptism, regarding Baptism as unnecessary. It is true that in some places sociological considerations associated with Baptism obscure its genuine meaning as an act of faith. This is due to a variety of historical and cultural factors which must be removed where they still exist, so that the sacrament of spiritual rebirth can be seen for what it truly is. Local ecclesial communities must devote themselves to this task. It is also true that many profess an interior commitment to Christ and his message yet do not wish to be committed sacramentally, since, owing to prejudice or because of the failings of Christians, they find it difficult to grasp the true nature of the Church as a mystery of faith and

63

love.[77] I wish to encourage such people to be fully open to Christ, and to remind them that, if they feel drawn to Christ, it was he himself who desired that the Church should be the "place" where they would in fact find him. At the same time, I invite the Christian faithful, both individually and as communities, to bear authentic witness to Christ through the new life they have received.

Certainly, every convert is a gift to the Church and represents a serious responsibility for her, not only because converts have to be prepared for Baptism through the catechumenate and then be guided by religious instruction, but also because—especially in the case of adults—such converts bring with them a kind of new energy, an enthusiasm for the faith, and a desire to see the Gospel lived out in the Church. They would be greatly disappointed if, having entered the ecclesial community, they were to find a life lacking fervor and without signs of renewal! We cannot preach conversion unless we ourselves are converted anew every day.

Forming Local Churches

48. Conversion and Baptism give entry into a Church already in existence or require the establishment of new communities which confess Jesus as Savior and Lord. This is part of God's plan, for it pleases him "to call human beings to share in his own life not merely as individuals, without any unifying bond between them, but rather to make them into a people in which his children, who had been widely scattered, might be gathered together in unity."[78]

The mission *ad gentes* has this objective: to found Christian communities and develop churches to their full maturity. This is a central and determining goal of missionary activity, so much so that the mission is not completed until it succeeds in building a new particular church which functions normally in its local setting. The Decree *Ad Gentes* deals with this subject at length,[79] and since the Council, a line of theological reflection has developed which emphasizes that the whole mystery of the Church is contained in each particular church, provided it does not isolate itself but remains in communion with the universal Church and becomes missionary in its own turn. Here we are speaking of a great and lengthy process, in which it is hard to identify the precise stage at which missionary activity properly so-called comes to an end and is replaced by pastoral activity. Even so, certain points must remain clear.

49. It is necessary first and foremost to strive to establish Christian communities everywhere, communities which are "a sign of the presence of God in the world"[80] and which grow until they become churches. Notwithstanding the high number of dioceses, there are still very large areas where there are no local churches or where their number is insufficient in relation to the vastness of the territory and the density of the population. There is still much to be done in implanting and developing the Church. This phase of ecclesial history, called the *plantatio Ecclesiae,* has not reached its end; indeed, for much of the human race it has yet to begin.

Responsibility for this task belongs to the universal Church and to the particular churches, to the whole people of God and to all its missionary forces. Every church, even one made up of recent converts, is missionary by its very nature, and is both evangelized and evangelizing. Faith must always be presented as a gift of God to be lived out in community (families, parishes, associations), and to be extended to others through witness in word and deed. The evangelizing activity of the Christian community, first in its own locality, and then elsewhere as part of the Church's universal mission, is the clearest sign of a mature faith. A radical conversion in thinking is required in order to become missionary, and this holds true both for individuals and entire communities. The Lord is always calling us to come out of ourselves and to share with others the goods we possess, starting with the most precious gift of all—our faith. The effectiveness of the Church's organizations, movements, parishes and apostolic works must be measured in the light of this missionary imperative. Only by becoming missionary will the Christian community be able to overcome its internal divisions and tensions, and rediscover its unity and its strength of faith.

Missionary personnel coming from other churches and countries must work in communion with their local counterparts for the development of the Christian community. In particular, it falls to missionary personnel—in accordance with the directives of the bishops and in cooperation with those responsible at the local level—to foster the spread of the faith and the expansion of the Church in non-Christian environments and among non-Christian groups, and to encourage a missionary sense within the particular churches, so that pastoral concern will always be combined with concern for the mission *ad gentes*. In this way, every church will make its own the solicitude of Christ the Good Shepherd, who fully devotes himself to his flock, but at the same time is mindful of the "other sheep, that are not of this fold" (Jn 10:16).

50. This solicitude will serve as a motivation and stimulus for a renewed commitment to ecumenism. The relationship between *ecumenical activity* and *missionary activity* makes it necessary to consider two closely associated factors. On the one hand, we must recognize that "the division among Christians damages the holy work of preaching the Gospel to every creature and is a barrier for many in their approach to the faith."[81] The fact that the Good News of reconciliation is preached by Christians who are divided among themselves

weakens their witness. It is thus urgent to work for the unity of Christians, so that missionary activity can be more effective. At the same time we must not forget that efforts toward unity are themselves a sign of the work of reconciliation which God is bringing about in our midst.

On the other hand, it is true that some kind of communion, though imperfect, exists among all those who have received Baptism in Christ. On this basis the Council established the principle that "while all appearance of indifferentism and confusion is ruled out, as well as any appearance of unhealthy rivalry, Catholics should collaborate in a spirit of fellowship with their separated brothers and sisters in accordance with the norms of the Decree on Ecumenism: by a common profession of faith in God and in Jesus Christ before the nations—to the extent that this is possible—and by their cooperation in social and technical as well as in cultural and religious matters."[82]

Ecumenical activity and harmonious witness to Jesus Christ by Christians who belong to different churches and ecclesial communities has already borne abundant fruit. But it is ever more urgent that they work and bear witness together at this time when Christian and para-Christian sects are sowing confusion by their activity. The expansion of these sects represents a threat for the Catholic Church and for all the ecclesial communities with which she is engaged in dialogue. Wherever possible, and in the light of local circumstances, the response of Christians can itself be an ecumenical one.

"Ecclesial Basic Communities"
As a Force for Evangelization

51. A rapidly growing phenomenon in the young churches—one sometimes fostered by the bishops and their Conferences as a pastoral priority—is that of "ecclesial basic

communities" (also known by other names) which are proving to be good centers for Christian formation and missionary outreach. These are groups of Christians who, at the level of the family or in a similarly restricted setting, come together for prayer, Scripture reading, catechesis, and discussion on human and ecclesial problems with a view to a common commitment. These communities are a sign of vitality within the Church, an instrument of formation and evangelization, and a solid starting point for a new society based on a "civilization of love."

These communities decentralize and organize the parish community, to which they always remain united. They take root in less privileged and rural areas, and become a leaven of Christian life, of care for the poor and neglected, and of commitment to the transformation of society. Within them, the individual Christian experiences community and therefore senses that he or she is playing an active role and is encouraged to share in the common task. Thus, these communities become a means of evangelization and of the initial proclamation of the Gospel, and a source of new ministries. At the same time, by being imbued with Christ's love, they also show how divisions, tribalism and racism can be overcome.

Every community, if it is to be Christian, must be founded on Christ and live in him, as it listens to the word of God, focuses its prayer on the Eucharist, lives in a communion marked by oneness of heart and soul, and shares according to the needs of its members (cf. Acts 2:42-47). As Pope Paul VI recalled, every community must live in union with the particular and the universal Church, in heartfelt communion with the Church's pastors and the Magisterium, with a commitment to missionary outreach and without yielding to isolationism or ideological exploitation.[83] And the Synod of Bishops stated: "Because the Church is communion, the new 'basic communities,' if they truly live in unity with the Church, are a true expression of communion and a means for the construction of a more profound communion. They are thus cause for great hope for the life of the Church."[84]

Incarnating the Gospel in Peoples' Cultures

52. As she carries out missionary activity among the nations, the Church encounters different cultures and becomes involved in the process of inculturation. The need for such involvement has marked the Church's pilgrimage throughout her history, but today it is particularly urgent.

The process of the Church's insertion into peoples' cultures is a lengthy one. It is not a matter of purely external adaptation, for inculturation "means the intimate transformation of authentic cultural values through their integration in Christianity and the insertion of Christianity in the various human cultures."[85] The process is thus a profound and all-embracing one, which involves the Christian message and also the Church's reflection and practice. But at the same time it is a difficult process, for it must in no way compromise the distinctiveness and integrity of the Christian faith.

Through inculturation the Church makes the Gospel incarnate in different cultures and at the same time introduces peoples, together with their cultures, into her own community.[86] She transmits to them her own values, at the same time taking the good elements that already exist in them and renewing them from within.[87] Through inculturation the Church, for her part, becomes a more intelligible sign of what she is, and a more effective instrument of mission.

Thanks to this action within the local churches, the universal Church herself is enriched with forms of expression and values in the various sectors of Christian life, such as evangelization, worship, theology and charitable works. She comes to know and to express better the mystery of Christ, all the while being motivated to continual renewal. During my pastoral visits to the young churches I have repeatedly dealt with these themes, which are present in the Council and the subsequent Magisterium.[88]

Inculturation is a slow journey which accompanies the whole of missionary life. It involves those working in the Church's mission *ad gentes,* the Christian communities as they develop, and the bishops, who have the task of providing discernment and encouragement for its implementation.[89]

53. Missionaries, who come from other churches and countries, must immerse themselves in the cultural milieu of those to whom they are sent, moving beyond their own cultural limitations. Hence they must learn the language of the place in which they work, become familiar with the most important expressions of the local culture, and discover its values through direct experience. Only if they have this kind of awareness will they be able to bring to people the knowledge of the hidden mystery (cf. Rom 16:25-27; Eph 3:5) in a credible and fruitful way. It is not of course a matter of missionaries renouncing their own cultural identity, but of understanding, appreciating, fostering and evangelizing the culture of the environment in which they are working, and therefore of equipping themselves to communicate effectively with it, adopting a manner of living which is a sign of gospel witness and of solidarity with the people.

Developing ecclesial communities, inspired by the Gospel, will gradually be able to express their Christian experience in original ways and forms that are consonant with their own cultural traditions, provided that those traditions are in harmony with the objective requirements of the faith itself. To this end, especially in the more delicate areas of inculturation, particular churches of the same region should work in communion with each other[90] and with the whole Church, convinced that only through attention both to the universal Church and to the particular churches will they be capable of translating the treasure of faith into a legitimate variety of expressions.[91] Groups which have been evangelized will thus provide the elements for a "translation" of the gospel message,[92] keeping in mind the positive elements acquired down the centuries from Christianity's contact with different cultures and not forgetting the dangers of alterations which have sometimes occurred.[93]

54. In this regard, certain guidelines remain basic. Properly applied, inculturation must be guided by two principles: "compatibility with the Gospel and communion with the universal Church."[94] Bishops, as guardians of the "deposit of faith," will take care to ensure fidelity and, in particular, to provide discernment,[95] for which a deeply balanced approach is required. In fact there is a risk of passing uncritically from a form of alienation from culture to an overestimation of culture. Since culture is a human creation and is therefore marked by sin, it too needs to be "healed, ennobled and perfected."[96]

This kind of process needs to take place gradually, in such a way that it really is an expression of the community's Christian experience. As Pope Paul VI said in Kampala: "It will require an incubation of the Christian 'mystery' in the genius of your people in order that its native voice, more clearly and frankly, may then be raised harmoniously in the chorus of other voices in the universal Church."[97] In effect, inculturation must involve the whole people of God, and not just a few experts, since the people reflect the authentic *sensus fidei* which must never be lost sight of. Inculturation needs to be guided and encouraged, but not forced, lest it give rise to negative reactions among Christians. It must be an expression of the community's life, one which must mature within the community itself, and not be exclusively the result of erudite research. The safeguarding of traditional values is the work of a mature faith.

Dialogue with Our Brothers and Sisters of Other Religions

55. Inter-religious dialogue is a part of the Church's evangelizing mission. Understood as a method and means of mutual knowledge and enrichment, dialogue is not in opposition to the mission *ad gentes;* indeed, it has special links with that mission and is one of its expressions. This mission, in fact, is addressed to those who do not know Christ and his Gospel, and who belong for the most part to other religions. In Christ, God calls all peoples to himself and he wishes to share with them the fullness of his revelation and love. He does not fail to make himself present in many ways, not only to individuals but also to entire peoples through their spiritual riches, of which their religions are the main and essential expression, even when they contain "gaps, insufficiencies and errors."[98] All of this has been given ample emphasis by the Council and the subsequent Magisterium, without detracting in any way from the fact that *salvation comes from Christ and that dialogue does not dispense from evangelization.*[99]

In the light of the economy of salvation, the Church sees no conflict between proclaiming Christ and engaging in inter-religious dialogue. Instead, she feels the need to link the two in the context of her mission *ad gentes.* These two elements must maintain both their intimate connection and their distinctiveness; therefore they should not be confused, manipulated or regarded as identical, as though they were interchangeable.

I recently wrote to the bishops of Asia: "Although the Church gladly acknowledges whatever is true and holy in the religious traditions of Buddhism, Hinduism and Islam as a reflection of that truth which enlightens all people, this does not lessen her duty and resolve to proclaim without fail Jesus Christ who is 'the way, and the truth and the life.'...The fact that the followers of other religions can receive God's grace and be saved by Christ apart from the ordinary means which he has established does not thereby cancel the call to faith and baptism which God wills for all people."[100] Indeed Christ himself "while expressly insisting on the need for faith and baptism, at the same time confirmed *the need for the Church,* into which people enter through Baptism as through a door."[101] Dialogue should be conducted and implemented with the conviction that *the Church is the ordinary means of salvation* and that *she alone* possesses the fullness of the means of salvation.[102]

56. Dialogue does not originate from tactical concerns or self-interest, but is an activity with its own guiding principles, requirements and dignity. It is demanded by deep respect for everything that has been brought about in human beings by the Spirit who blows where he wills.[103] Through dialogue, the Church seeks to uncover the "seeds of the Word,"[104] a "ray of that truth which enlightens all men";[105] these are found in individuals and in the religious traditions of mankind. Dialogue is based on hope and love, and will bear fruit in the Spirit. Other religions constitute a positive challenge for the Church: they stimulate her both to discover and acknowledge the signs of Christ's presence and of the working of the Spirit, as well as to examine more deeply her own identity and to bear witness to the fullness of Revelation which she has received for the good of all.

This gives rise to the spirit which must enliven dialogue in the context of mission. Those engaged in this dialogue must be consistent with their own religious traditions and convictions, and be open to understanding those of the other party without pretense or close-mindedness, but with truth, humility and frankness, knowing that dialogue can enrich each side. There must be no abandonment of principles nor false irenicism, but instead a witness given and received for mutual advancement on the road of religious inquiry and experience, and at the same time for the elimination of prejudice, intolerance and misunderstandings. Dialogue leads to inner purification and conversion which, if pursued with docility to the Holy Spirit, will be spiritually fruitful.

57. A vast field lies open to dialogue, which can assume many forms and expressions: from exchanges between experts in religious traditions or official representatives of those traditions to cooperation for integral development and the safeguarding of religious values; and from a sharing of their respective spiritual experiences to the so-called "dialogue of life," through which believers of different religions bear witness before each other in daily life to their own human and spiritual values, and help each other to live according to those values in order to build a more just and fraternal society.

Each member of the faithful and all Christian communities are called to practice dialogue, although not always to the same degree or in the same way. The contribution of the laity is indispensable in this area, for they "can favor the relations which ought to be established with the followers of various religions through their example in the situations in which they live and in their activities."[106] Some of them also will be able to make a contribution through research and study.[107]

I am well aware that many missionaries and Christian communities find in the difficult and often misunderstood path of dialogue their only way of bearing sincere witness to Christ and offering generous service to others. I wish to encourage them to persevere with faith and love, even in places where their efforts are not well received. Dialogue is a path toward the kingdom and will certainly bear fruit, even if the times and seasons are known only to the Father (cf. Acts 1:7).

Promoting Development by Forming Consciences

58. The mission *ad gentes* is still being carried out today, for the most part in the southern regions of the world, where action on behalf of integral development and liberation from all forms of oppression is most urgently needed. The Church has always been able to generate among the peoples she evangelizes a drive toward progress. Today, more than in the past, missionaries are being recognized as *promoters of development* by governments and international experts who are impressed at the remarkable results achieved with scanty means.

In the Encyclical *Sollicitudo Rei Socialis,* I stated that "the Church does not have technical solutions to offer for the problem of underdevelopment as such," but "offers her first contribution to the solution of the urgent problem of development when she proclaims the truth about Christ, about herself and about man, applying this truth to a concrete situation."[108] The Conference of Latin American Bishops at Puebla stated that "the best service we can offer to our brother is evangelization, which helps him to live and act as a son of God, sets him free from injustices and assists his overall development."[109] It is not the Church's mission to work directly on the economic, technical or political levels, or to contribute materially to development. Rather, her mission consists essentially in offering people an opportunity not to "have more" but to "be more," by awakening their consciences through the Gospel. "Authentic human development must be rooted in an ever deeper evangelization."[110]

The Church and her missionaries also promote development through schools, hospitals, printing presses, universities and experimental farms. But a people's development does not derive primarily from money, material assistance or technological means, but from the formation of consciences and the gradual maturing of ways of thinking and patterns of behavior. *Man is the principle agent of development,* not money or technology. The Church forms consciences by revealing to peoples the God whom they seek and do not yet know, the grandeur of man created in God's image and loved by him, the equality of all men and women as God's sons and daughters, the mastery of man over nature created by God and placed at man's service, and the obligation to work for the development of the whole person and of all mankind.

59. Through the gospel message, the Church offers a force for liberation which promotes development precisely because it leads to conversion of heart and of ways of thinking, fosters the recognition of each person's dignity, encourages solidarity, commitment and service of one's neighbor, and gives everyone a place in God's plan, which is the building of his kingdom of peace and justice, beginning already in this life. This is the biblical perspective of the "new heavens and a new earth" (cf. Is 65:17; 2 Pt 3:13; Rv 21:1), which has been the stimulus and goal for mankind's advancement in history. Man's development derives from God, and from the model of Jesus—God and man—and must lead back to God.[111] That is why there is a close connection between the proclamation of the Gospel and human promotion.

The contribution of the Church and of evagelization to the development of peoples concerns not only the struggle against material poverty and underdevelopment in the South of the world, but also concerns the North, which is prone to a moral and spiritual poverty caused by "overdevelopment."[112] A certain way of thinking, uninfluenced by a religious outlook and widespread in some parts of today's world, is based on the idea that increasing wealth and the promotion of economic and technical growth is enough for people to develop on the human level. But a soulless development cannot suffice for human beings, and an excess of affluence is as harmful as excessive poverty. This is a "development model" which the North has constructed and is now spreading to the South, where a sense of religion as well as human values are in danger of being overwhelmed by a wave of consumerism.

"Fight hunger by changing your lifestyle" is a motto which has appeared in Church circles and which shows the people of the rich nations how to become brothers and sisters of the poor. We need to turn to a more austere way of life which will favor a new model of development that gives attention to ethical and religious values. To the poor, *missionary activity* brings light and an impulse toward true development, while a new evangelization ought to create among the wealthy a realization that the time has arrived for them to become true brothers and sisters of the poor through the conversion of all to an "integral development" open to the Absolute.[113]

Charity: Source and Criterion of Mission

60. As I said during my pastoral visit to Brazil: "The Church all over the world wishes to be the Church of the poor...she wishes to draw out all the truth contained in the Beatitudes of Christ, and especially in the first one: 'Blessed are the poor in spirit.' ...She wishes to teach this truth and she wishes to put it into practice, just as Jesus came to do and to teach."[114]

The young churches, which for the most part are to be found among peoples suffering from widespread poverty, often give voice to this concern as an integral part of their mission. The Conference of Latin American Bishops at Puebla, after recalling the example of Jesus, wrote that "the poor deserve preferential attention, whatever their moral or personal situation. They have been made in the image and likeness of God to be his children, but this image has been obscured and even violated. For this reason, God has become their defender and loves them. It follows that the poor are those to whom the mission is first addressed, and their evangelization is *par excellence* the sign and proof of the mission of Jesus."[115]

In fidelity to the spirit of the Beatitudes, the Church is called to be on the side of those who are poor and oppressed in any way. I therefore exhort the disciples of Christ and all Christian communities—from families to dioceses, from parishes to religious institutes—to carry out a sincere review of their lives regarding their solidarity with the poor. At the same time, I express gratitude to the missionaries who, by their loving presence and humble service to people, are working for the integral development of individuals and of society through schools, health-care centers, leprosaria, homes for the handicapped and the elderly, projects for the promotion of women, and other similar apostolates. I thank the priests, religious brothers and sisters, and members of the laity for their dedication, and I also encourage the volunteers from non-governmental organizations who in ever increasing numbers are devoting themselves to works of charity and human promotion.

It is in fact these "works of charity" that reveal the soul of all missionary activity: *love,* which has been and remains *the driving force of mission,* and is also "the sole criterion for judging what is to be done or not done, changed or not changed. It is the principle which must direct every action, and the end to which that action must be directed. When we act with a view to charity, or are inspired by charity, nothing is unseemly and everything is good."[116]

Chapter VI

Leaders and Workers
in the Missionary Apostolate

61. Without witnesses there can be no witness, just as without missionaries there can be no missionary activity. Jesus chooses and sends people forth to be his witnesses and apostles, so that they may share in his mission and continue in his saving work: "You shall be my witnesses in Jerusalem and in all Judea and Samaria and to the end of the earth" (Acts 1:8).

The Twelve are the first to work in the Church's universal mission. They constitute a "collegial subject" of that mission, having been chosen by Jesus to be with him and to be sent forth "to the lost sheep of the house of Israel" (Mt 10:6). This collegiality does not prevent certain figures from assuming prominence within the group, such as James, John and above all Peter, who is so prominent as to justify the expression: "Peter and the other Apostles" (Acts 2:14, 37). It was thanks to Peter that the horizons of the Church's universal mission were expanded, and the way was prepared for the outstanding missionary work of Paul, who by God's will was called and sent forth to the nations (cf. Gal 1:15-16).

In the early Church's missionary expansion, we find alongside the apostles, other lesser figures who should not be overlooked. These include individuals, groups and communities. A typical example is the local church at Antioch which, after being evangelized, becomes an evangelizing community which sends missionaries to others (cf. Acts 13:2-3). The early Church experiences her mission as a community task, while acknowledging in her midst certain "special envoys" or "missionaries devoted to the Gentiles," such as Paul and Barnabas.

62. What was done at the beginning of Christianity to further its universal mission remains valid and urgent today. *The Church is missionary by her very nature,* for Christ's mandate is not something contingent or external, but reaches the very heart of the Church. It follows that the universal Church and each individual church is sent forth to the nations. Precisely "so that this missionary zeal may flourish among the people of their own country," it is highly appropriate that young churches should "share as soon as possible in the universal missionary work of the Church. They should themselves send missionaries to proclaim the Gospel all over the world, even though they are suffering from a shortage of clergy."[117] Many are already doing so, and I strongly encourage them to continue.

In this essential bond between the universal Church and the particular churches the authentic and full missionary nature of the Church finds practical expression: "In a world where the lessening of distance makes the world increasingly smaller, the Church's communities ought to be connected with each other, exchange vital energies and resources, and commit themselves as a group to the one and common mission of proclaiming and living the Gospel.... So-called younger churches have need of the strength of the older churches and the older ones need the witness and the impulse of the younger, so that each church can draw on the riches of the other churches."[118]

Those Primarily Responsible for Missionary Activity

63. Just as the risen Lord gave the universal missionary mandate to the College of the Apostles with Peter as its head, so this same responsibility now rests primarily with the College of Bishops, headed by the successor of Peter.[119] Conscious of this responsibility, I feel the duty to give expression to it in my meetings with the bishops, both with regard to new evangelization and the universal mission. I have traveled all over the world in order "to proclaim the Gospel, to 'strengthen the brothers' in the faith, to console the Church, to meet people. They are journeys of faith...they are likewise opportunities for traveling catechesis, for evangelical proclamation in spreading the Gospel and the apostolic Magisterium to the full extent of the world."[120]

My brother bishops are directly responsible, together with me, for the evangelization of the world, both as members of the College of Bishops and as pastors of the particular churches. In this regard the Council states: "The charge of announcing the Gospel throughout the world belongs to the body of shepherds, to all of whom in common Christ gave the command."[121] It also stated that the bishops "have been consecrated not only for a particular diocese but for the salvation of the entire world."[122] This collegial responsibility has certain practical consequences. Thus, "the Synod of Bishops ...should, among the concerns of general importance, pay special attention to missionary activity, the greatest and holiest duty of the Church."[123] The same responsibility is reflected to varying degrees in Episcopal Conferences and their organisms at a continental level, which must make their own contribution to the missionary task.[124]

Each bishop too, as the pastor of a particular church, has a wide-ranging missionary duty. It falls to him "as the ruler and center of unity in the diocesan apostolate, to promote missionary activity, to direct and coordinate it…. Let him also see to it that apostolic activity is not limited only to those who are already converted, but that a fair share both of personnel and funds be devoted to the evangelization of non-Christians."[125]

64. Each particular church must be generous and open to the needs of the other churches. Cooperation between the churches, in an authentic reciprocity that prepares them both to give and to receive, is a source of enrichment for all of them and touches the various spheres of ecclesial life. In this respect, the declaration of the bishops at Puebla is exemplary: "The hour has finally come for Latin America…to be projected beyond her frontiers, *ad gentes.* Certainly we have need of missionaries ourselves, nevertheless we must give from our own poverty."[126]

In the same spirit, I exhort bishops and Episcopal Conferences to act generously in implementing the provisions of the *norms* which the Congregation for the Clergy issued regarding cooperation between particular churches and especially regarding the better distribution of clergy in the world.[127]

The Church's mission is wider than the "communion among the churches"; it ought to be directed not only to aiding re-evangelization but also and primarily to missionary activity as such. I appeal to all the churches, young and old alike, to share in this concern of mine by seeking to overcome the various obstacles and increase missionary vocations.

Missionaries and Religious Institutes Ad Gentes

65. Now, as in the past, among those involved in the missionary apostolate a place of fundamental importance is

held by the persons and institutions to whom the Decree *Ad Gentes* devotes the special chapter entitled "Missionaries."[128] This requires careful reflection, especially on the part of missionaries themselves, who may be led, as a result of changes occurring within the missionary field, no longer to understand the meaning of their vocation and no longer to know exactly what the Church expects of them today.

The following words of the Council are a point of reference: "Although the task of spreading the faith, to the best of one's ability, falls to each disciple of Christ, the Lord always calls from the number of his disciples those whom he wishes, so that they may be with him and that he may send them to preach to the nations. Accordingly, through the Holy Spirit, who distributes his gifts as he wishes for the good of all, Christ stirs up a missionary vocation in the hearts of individuals, and at the same time raises up in the Church those institutes which undertake the duty of evangelization, which is the responsibility of the whole Church, as their special task."[129]

What is involved, therefore, is a "special vocation," patterned on that of the apostles. It is manifested in a total commitment to evangelization, a commitment which involves the missionary's whole person and life, and demands a self-giving without limits of energy or time. Those who have received this vocation, "sent by legitimate authority, go out, in faith and obedience, to those who are far from Christ, set aside for the work to which they have been called as ministers of the Gospel."[130] Missionaries must always meditate on the response demanded by the gift they have received, and continually keep their doctrinal and apostolic formation up to date.

66. Missionary institutes, drawing from their experience and creativity while remaining faithful to their founding

charism, must employ all means necessary to ensure the adequate preparation of candidates and the renewal of their members' spiritual, moral and physical energies.[131] They should sense that they are a vital part of the ecclesial community and should carry out their work in communion with it. Indeed, "every institute exists for the Church and must enrich her with its distinctive characteristics, according to a particular spirit and a specific mission"; the guardians of this fidelity to the founding charism are the bishops themselves.[132]

In general, missionary institutes came into being in churches located in traditionally Christian countries, and historically they have been the means employed by the Congregation of *Propaganda Fide* for the spread of the faith and the founding of new churches. Today, these institutes are receiving more and more candidates from the young churches which they founded, while new missionary institutes have arisen in countries which previously only received missionaries, but are now also sending them. This is a praiseworthy trend which demonstrates the continuing validity and relevance of the specific missionary vocation of these institutes. They remain "absolutely necessary,"[133] not only for missionary activity *ad gentes,* in keeping with their tradition, but also for stirring up missionary fervor both in the churches of traditionally Christian countries and in the younger churches.

The special vocation of missionaries *"for life"* retains all its validity: it is the model of the Church's missionary commitment, which always stands in need of radical and total self-giving, of new and bold endeavors. Therefore the men and women missionaries who have devoted their whole lives to bearing witness to the risen Lord among the nations must not allow themselves to be daunted by doubts, misunderstanding, rejection or persecution. They should revive the grace of their specific charism and courageously press on, preferring—in a spirit of faith, obedience and communion with their pastors— to seek the lowliest and most demanding places.

Diocesan Priests for the Universal Mission

67. As co-workers of the bishops, priests are called by virtue of the sacrament of Orders to share in concern for the Church's mission: "The spiritual gift that priests have received in ordination prepares them, not for any narrow and limited mission, but for *the most universal and all embracing mission of salvation* 'to the end of the earth.' For every priestly ministry shares in the universal scope of the mission that Christ entrusted to his apostles."[134] For this reason, the formation of candidates to the priesthood must aim at giving them *"the true Catholic spirit,* whereby they will learn to transcend the bounds of their own diocese, country or rite, and come to the aid of the whole Church, in readiness to preach the Gospel anywhere."[135] All priests must have the mind and the heart of missionaries—open to the needs of the Church and the world, with concern for those farthest away, and especially for the non-Christian groups in their own area. They should have at heart, in their prayers and particularly at the Eucharistic Sacrifice, the concern of the whole Church for all of humanity.

Especially in those areas where Christians are a minority, priests must be filled with special missionary zeal and commitment. The Lord entrusts to them not only the pastoral care of the Christian community, but also and above all the evangelization of those of their fellow-citizens who do not belong to Christ's flock. Priests will "not fail to make themselves readily available to the Holy Spirit and the bishop, to be sent to preach the Gospel beyond the borders of their country. This will demand of them not only maturity in their vocation, but also an uncommon readiness to detach themselves from their own homeland, culture and family, and a special ability to adapt to other cultures, with understanding and respect for them."[136]

68. In his Encyclical *Fidei Donum,* Pope Pius XII, with prophetic insight, encouraged bishops to offer some of their priests for temporary service in the churches of Africa, and gave his approval to projects already existing for that purpose. Twenty-five years later, I pointed out the striking newness of that encyclical, which "surmounted the territorial dimension of priestly service in order to direct it toward the entire Church."[137] Today it is clear how effective and fruitful this experience has been. Indeed, *Fidei Donum* priests are a unique sign of the bond of communion existing among the churches. They make a valuable contribution to the growth of needy ecclesial communities, while drawing from them freshness and liveliness of faith. Of course, the missionary service of the diocesan priest must conform to certain criteria and conditions. The priests to be sent should be selected from among the most suitable candidates, and should be duly prepared for the particular work that awaits them.[138] With an open and fraternal attitude, they should become part of the new setting of the Church which welcomes them, and form one presbyterate with the local priests, under the authority of the bishop.[139] I hope that a spirit of service will increase among the priests of the long-established churches, and that it will be fostered among priests of the churches of more recent origin.

The Missionary Fruitfulness of Consecrated Life

69. From the inexhaustible and manifold richness of the Spirit come the vocations of the *Institutes of Consecrated Life,* whose members, "because of the dedication to the service of the Church deriving from their very consecration, have an

obligation to play a special part in missionary activity, in a manner appropriate to their Institute."[140] History witnesses to the outstanding service rendered by religious families in the spread of the faith and the formation of new churches: from the ancient monastic institutions, to the medieval Orders, up to the more recent congregations.

(a) Echoing the Council, I invite *institutes of contemplative life* to establish communities in the young churches, so as to "bear glorious witness among non-Christians to the majesty and love of God, as well as to unity in Christ."[141] This presence is beneficial throughout the non-Christian world, especially in those areas where religious traditions hold the contemplative life in great esteem for its asceticism and its search for the Absolute.

(b) To *institutes of active life,* I would recommend the immense opportunities for works of charity, for the proclamation of the Gospel, for Christian education, cultural endeavors and solidarity with the poor and those suffering from discrimination, abandonment and oppression. Whether they pursue a strictly missionary goal or not, such institutes should ask themselves how willing and able they are to broaden their action in order to extend God's kingdom. In recent times many institutes have responded to this request, which I hope will be given even greater consideration and implementation for a more authentic service. The Church needs to make known the great gospel values of which she is the bearer. No one witnesses more effectively to these values than those who profess the consecrated life in chastity, poverty and obedience, in a total gift of self to God and in complete readiness to serve humanity and society after the example of Christ.[142]

70. I extend a special word of appreciation to the missionary religious sisters, in whom virginity for the sake of the kingdom is transformed into a motherhood in the spirit that

is rich and fruitful. It is precisely the mission *ad gentes* that offers them vast scope for "the gift of self with love in a total and undivided manner."[143] The example and activity of women who through virginity are consecrated to love of God and neighbor, especially the very poor, are an indispensable evangelical sign among those peoples and cultures where women still have far to go on the way toward human promotion and liberation. It is my hope that many young Christian women will be attracted to giving themselves generously to Christ, and will draw strength and joy from their consecration in order to bear witness to him among the peoples who do not know him.

All the Laity Are Missionaries by Baptism

71. Recent popes have stressed the importance of the role of the laity in missionary activity.[144] In the Exhortation *Christifideles Laici,* I spoke explicitly of the Church's "permanent mission of bringing the Gospel to the multitudes—the millions and millions of men and women—who as yet do not know Christ the Redeemer of humanity,"[145] and of the responsibility of the lay faithful in this regard. The mission *ad gentes* is incumbent upon the entire People of God. Whereas the foundation of a new church requires the Eucharist and hence the priestly ministry, missionary activity, which is carried out in a wide variety of ways, is the task of all the Christian faithful.

It is clear that from the very origins of Christianity, the laity—as individuals, families, and entire communities—shared in spreading the faith. Pope Pius XII recalled this fact in his first encyclical on the missions,[146] in which he pointed out some instances of lay missions. In modern times, this active participation of lay men and women missionaries has not been lacking. How can we forget the important role played by women: their work in the family, in schools, in political, social and cultural life, and especially their teaching of Christian doctrine? Indeed, it is necessary to recognize—and it is a title of honor—that some churches owe their origins to the activity of lay men and women missionaries.

The Second Vatican Council confirmed this tradition in its description of the missionary character of the entire People of God and of the apostolate of the laity in particular,[147] emphasizing the specific contribution to missionary activity which they are called to make.[148] The need for all the faithful to share in this responsibility is not merely a matter of making the apostolate more effective; it is a right and duty based on their baptismal dignity, whereby "the faithful participate, for their part, in the threefold mission of Christ as Priest, Prophet and King."[149] Therefore, "they are bound by the general obligation and they have the right, whether as individuals or in associations, to strive so that the divine message of salvation may be known and accepted by all people throughout the world. This obligation is all the more insistent in circumstances in which only through them are people able to hear the Gospel and to know Christ."[150] Furthermore, because of their secular character, they especially are called "to seek the kingdom of God by engaging in temporal affairs and ordering these in accordance with the will of God."[151]

72. The sphere in which lay people are present and active as missionaries is very extensive. "Their own field...is the vast and complicated world of politics, society and economics..."[152] on the local, national and international levels. Within the Church, there are various types of services, functions, ministries and ways of promoting the Christian life. I call to mind, as a new development occurring in many churches in recent times, the rapid growth of "ecclesial

movements" filled with missionary dynamism. When these movements humbly seek to become part of the life of local churches and are welcomed by bishops and priests within diocesan and parish structures, they represent a true gift of God both for new evangelization and for missionary activity properly so-called. I therefore recommend that they be spread, and that they be used to give fresh energy, especially among young people, to the Christian life and to evangelization, within a pluralistic view of the ways in which Christians can associate and express themselves.

Within missionary activity, the different forms of the lay apostolate should be held in esteem, with respect for their nature and aims. Lay missionary associations, international Christian volunteer organizations, ecclesial movements, groups and solidarities of different kinds—all these should be involved in the mission *ad gentes* as cooperators with the local churches. In this way the growth of a mature and responsible laity will be fostered, a laity whom the younger churches are recognizing as "an essential and undeniable element in the *plantatio Ecclesiae.*"[153]

The Work of Catechists and the Variety of Ministries

73. Among the laity who become evangelizers, catechists have a place of honor. The Decree on the Missionary Activity of the Church speaks of them as "that army of catechists, both men and women, worthy of praise, to whom missionary work among the nations owes so much. Imbued with the apostolic spirit, they make a singular and absolutely necessary contribution to the spread of the faith and of the Church by their strenuous efforts."[154] It is with good reason that the older and established churches, committed to a new evangelization, have increased the numbers of their catechists and intensified

catechetical activity. But "the term 'catechists' belongs above all to the catechists in mission lands.... Churches that are flourishing today would not have been built up without them."[155]

Even with the extension of the services rendered by lay people both within and outside the Church, there is always need for the ministry of catechists, a ministry with its own characteristics. Catechists are specialists, direct witnesses and irreplaceable evangelizers who, as I have often stated and experienced during my missionary journeys, represent the basic strength of Christian communities, especially in the young churches. The new Code of Canon Law acknowledges the tasks, qualities and qualifications of catechists.[156]

However, it must not be forgotten that the work of catechists is becoming more and more difficult and demanding as a result of ecclesial and cultural changes. What the Council suggested is still valid today: a more careful doctrinal and pedagogical training, continuing spiritual and apostolic renewal, and the need to provide "a decent standard of living and social security."[157] It is also important to make efforts to establish and support schools for catechists, which are to be approved by the Episcopal Conferences and confer diplomas officially recognized by the latter.[158]

74. Besides catechists, mention must also be made of other ways of serving the Church and her mission; namely, other Church personnel: leaders of prayer, song and liturgy; leaders of basic ecclesial communities and Bible study groups; those in charge of charitable works; administrators of Church resources; leaders in the various forms of the apostolate; religion teachers in schools. All the members of the laity ought to devote a part of their time to the Church, living their faith authentically.

The Congregation for the Evangelization of Peoples and Other Structures for Missionary Activity

75. Leaders and agents of missionary pastoral activity should sense their unity within the communion which characterizes the Mystical Body. Christ prayed for this at the Last Supper when he said: "Even as you, Father, are in me, and I in you, that they also may be in us, so that the world may believe that you have sent me" (Jn 17:21). The fruitfulness of missionary activity is to be found in this communion.

But since the Church is also a communion which is visible and organic, her mission requires an external and ordered union between the various responsibilities and functions involved, in such a way that all the members "may in harmony spend their energies for the building up of the Church."[159]

To the congregation responsible for missionary activity it falls "to direct and coordinate throughout the world the work of evangelizing peoples and of missionary cooperation, with due regard for the competence of the Congregation for the Oriental Churches."[160] Hence, its task is to "recruit missionaries and distribute them in accordance with the more urgent needs of various regions...draw up an ordered plan of action, issue norms and directives, as well as principles which are appropriate for the work of evangelization, and assist in the initial stages of their work."[161] I can only confirm these wise directives. In order to re-launch the mission *ad gentes,* a center of outreach, direction and coordination is needed, namely, the Congregation for the Evangelization of Peoples. I invite the Episcopal Conferences and their various bodies, the major superiors of orders, congregations and institutes, as well as lay organizations involved in missionary activity, to cooperate faithfully with this Dicastery, which has the authority necessary to plan and direct missionary activity and cooperation worldwide.

The same congregation, which has behind it a long and illustrious history, is called to play a role of primary importance with regard to reflection and programs of action which the Church needs in order to be more decisively oriented toward the mission in its various forms. To this end, the congregation should maintain close relations with the other Dicasteries of the Holy See, with the local churches and the various missionary forces. In an ecclesiology of communion in which the entire Church is missionary, but in which specific vocations and institutions for missionary work *ad gentes* remains indispensable, the guiding and coordinating role of the Congregation for the Evangelization of Peoples remains very important in order to ensure a united effort in confronting great questions of common concern, with due regard for the competence proper to each authority and structure.

76. Episcopal Conferences and their various groupings have great importance in directing and coordinating missionary activity on the national and regional levels. The Council asks them to "confer together in dealing with more important questions and urgent problems, without, however, overlooking local differences,"[162] and to consider the complex issue of inculturation. In fact, large-scale and regular activity is already taking place in this area, with visible results. It is an activity which must be intensified and better coordinated with that of other bodies of the same Conferences, so that missionary concern will not be left to the care of only one sector or body, but will be shared by all.

The bodies and institutions involved in missionary activity should join forces and initiatives as opportunity suggests. Conferences of Major Superiors should have this same concern in their own sphere, maintaining contact with Episcopal

Conferences in accordance with established directives and norms,[163] and also having recourse to mixed commissions.[164] Also desirable are meetings and other forms of cooperation between the various missionary institutions, both in formation and study,[165] as well as in the actual apostolate.

Chapter VII

Cooperation in Missionary Activity

77. Since they are members of the Church by virtue of their Baptism, all Christians share responsibility for missionary activity. "Missionary cooperation" is the expression used to describe the sharing by communities and individual Christians in this right and duty.

Missionary cooperation is rooted and lived, above all, in personal union with Christ. Only if we are united to him as the branches to the vine (cf. Jn 15:5) can we produce good fruit. Through holiness of life every Christian can become a fruitful part of the Church's mission. The Second Vatican Council invited all "to a profound interior renewal, so that having a lively awareness of their personal responsibility for the spreading of the Gospel, they may play their part in missionary work among the nations."[166]

Sharing in the universal mission therefore is not limited to certain specific activities, but is the sign of maturity in faith and of a Christian life that bears fruit. In this way, individual believers extend the reach of their charity and show concern for those both far and near. They pray for the missions and missionary vocations. They help missionaries and follow their work with interest. And when missionaries return, they welcome them with the same joy with which the first Christian communities heard from the apostles the marvelous things which God had wrought through their preaching (cf. Acts 14:27).

Prayer and Sacrifice for Missionaries

78. Among the forms of sharing, first place goes to spiritual cooperation through prayer, sacrifice and the witness of Christian life. Prayer should accompany the journey of missionaries so that the proclamation of the word will be effective through God's grace. In his Letters, St. Paul often asks the faithful to pray for him so that he might proclaim the Gospel with confidence and conviction. Prayer needs to be accompanied by sacrifice. The redemptive value of suffering, accepted and offered to God with love, derives from the sacrifice of Christ himself, who calls the members of his Mystical Body to share in his sufferings, to complete them in their own flesh (cf. Col 1:24). The sacrifice of missionaries should be shared and accompanied by the sacrifices of all the faithful. I therefore urge those engaged in the pastoral care of the sick to teach them about the efficacy of suffering, and to encourage them to offer their sufferings to God for missionaries. By making such an offering, the sick themselves become missionaries, as emphasized by a number of movements which have sprung up among them and for them. The solemnity of Pentecost—the beginning of the Church's mission—is celebrated in some communities as a "Day of Suffering for the Missions."

"Here I am, Lord! I am ready! Send me!" (cf. Is 6:8)

79. Cooperation is expressed above all by promoting missionary vocations. While acknowledging the validity of various ways of being involved in missionary activity, it is necessary at the same time to reaffirm that *a full and lifelong commitment to the work of the missions holds pride of place,* especially in missionary institutes and congregations. Promot-

ing such vocations is at the heart of missionary cooperation. Preaching the Gospel requires preachers; the harvest needs laborers. The mission is carried out above all by men and women who are consecrated for life to the work of the Gospel and are prepared to go forth into the whole world to bring salvation.

I wish to call to mind and to recommend this *concern for missionary vocations.* Conscious of the overall responsibility of Christians to contribute to missionary activity and to the development of poorer peoples, we must ask ourselves how it is that in some countries, while monetary contributions are on the increase, missionary vocations, which are the real measure of self-giving to one's brothers and sisters, are in danger of disappearing. Vocations to the priesthood and the consecrated life are a sure sign of the vitality of a church.

80. As I think of this serious problem, I appeal with great confidence and affection to families and to young people. Families, especially parents, should be conscious that they ought to "offer a special contribution to the missionary cause of the Church by fostering missionary vocations among their sons and daughters."[167]

An intense prayer life, a genuine sense of service to one's neighbor and a generous participation in Church activities provide families with conditions that favor vocations among young people. When parents are ready to allow one of their children to leave for the missions, when they have sought this grace from the Lord, he will repay them, in joy, on the day that their son or daughter hears his call.

I ask young people themselves to listen to Christ's words as he says to them what he once said to Simon Peter and to Andrew at the lakeside: "Follow me, and I will make you fishers of men" (Mt 4:19). May they have the courage to reply as Isaiah did: "Here am I, Lord! I am ready! Send me!"

(cf. Is 6:8) They will have a wonderful life ahead of them, and they will know the genuine joy of proclaiming the "Good News" to brothers and sisters whom they will lead on the way of salvation.

"It is more blessed to give than to receive" *(Acts 20:35)*

81. The material and financial needs of the missions are many: not only to set up the Church with minimal structures (chapels, schools for catechists and seminarians, housing), but also to support works of charity, education and human promotion—a vast field of action especially in poor countries. The missionary Church gives what she receives, and distributes to the poor the material goods that her materially richer sons and daughters generously put at her disposal. Here I wish to thank all those who make sacrifices and contribute to the work of the missions. Their sacrifices and sharing are indispensable for building up the Church and for showing love.

In the matter of material help, it is important to consider the spirit in which donations are made. For this we should re-assess our own way of living: the missions ask not only for a contribution but for a sharing in the work of preaching and charity toward the poor. All that we have received from God—life itself as well as material goods—does not belong to us but is given to us for our use. Generosity in giving must always be enlightened and inspired by faith: then we will truly be more blessed in giving than in receiving.

World Mission Day, which seeks to heighten awareness of the missions, as well as to collect funds for them, is an important date in the life of the Church, because it teaches how to give: as an offering made to God, *in* the Eucharistic celebration and *for* all the missions of the world.

New Forms of Missionary Cooperation

82. Today, cooperation includes new forms—not only economic assistance, but also direct participation. New situations connected with the phenomenon of mobility demand from Christians an authentic missionary spirit.

International tourism has now become a mass phenomenon. This is a positive development if tourists maintain an attitude of respect and a desire for mutual cultural enrichment, avoiding ostentation and waste, and seeking contact with other people. But Christians are expected above all to be aware of their obligation to bear witness always to their faith and love of Christ. Firsthand knowledge of the missionary life and of new Christian communities also can be an enriching experience and can strengthen one's faith. Visiting the missions is commendable, especially on the part of young people who go there to serve and to gain an intense experience of the Christian life.

Reasons of work nowadays bring many Christians from young communities to areas where Christianity is unknown and at times prohibited or persecuted. The same is true of members of the faithful from traditionally Christian countries who work for a time in non-Christian countries. These circumstances are certainly an opportunity to live the faith and to bear witness to it. In the early centuries, Christianity spread because Christians, traveling to or settling in regions where Christ had not yet been proclaimed, bore courageous witness to their faith and founded the first communities there.

More numerous are the citizens of mission countries and followers of non-Christian religions who settle in other nations for reasons of study or work, or are forced to do so because of the political or economic situations in their native lands. The presence of these brothers and sisters in traditionally

Christian countries is a challenge for the ecclesial communities, and a stimulus to hospitality, dialogue, service, sharing, witness and direct proclamation. In Christian countries, communities and cultural groups are also forming which call for the mission *ad gentes,* and the local churches, with the help of personnel from the immigrants' own countries and of returning missionaries, should respond generously to these situations.

Missionary cooperation can also involve leaders in politics, economics, culture and journalism, as well as experts of the various international bodies. In the modern world it is becoming increasingly difficult to determine geographical or cultural boundaries. There is an increasing interdependence between peoples, and this constitutes a stimulus for Christian witness and evangelization.

Missionary Promotion and Formation Among the People of God

83. Missionary formation is the task of the local Church, assisted by missionaries and their institutes, and by personnel from the young churches. This work must be seen not as peripheral but as central to the Christian life. Even for the "new evangelization" of Christian countries the theme of the missions can prove very helpful: the witness of missionaries retains its appeal even for the non-practicing and non-believers, and it communicates Christian values. Particular churches should therefore make the promotion of the missions a key element in the normal pastoral activity of parishes, associations and groups, especially youth groups.

With this end in view, it is necessary to spread information through missionary publications and audiovisual aids. These play an important role in making known the life of the universal Church and in voicing the experiences of missionaries and of the local churches in which they work. In those younger churches which are still not able to have a press and other means of their own, it is important that missionary institutes devote personnel and resources to these undertakings.

Such formation is entrusted to priests and their associates, to educators and teachers, and to theologians, particularly those who teach in seminaries and centers for the laity. Theological training cannot and should not ignore the Church's universal mission, ecumenism, the study of the great religions and missiology. I recommend that such studies be undertaken especially in seminaries and in houses of formation for men and women religious, ensuring that some priests or other students specialize in the different fields of missiology.

Activities aimed at promoting interest in the missions must always be geared to these specific goals; namely, informing and forming the People of God to share in the Church's universal mission, promoting vocations *ad gentes* and encouraging cooperation in the work of evangelization. It is not right to give an incomplete picture of missionary activity, as if it consisted principally in helping the poor, contributing to the liberation of the oppressed, promoting development or defending human rights. The missionary Church is certainly involved on these fronts but her primary task lies elsewhere: the poor are hungry for God, not just for bread and freedom. Missionary activity must first of all bear witness to and proclaim salvation in Christ, and establish local churches which then become means of liberation in every sense.

The Primary Responsibility of the Pontifical Mission Societies

84. The leading role in this work of promotion belongs to the *Pontifical Mission Societies,* as I have often pointed out

in my Messages for World Mission Day. The four Societies—Propagation of the Faith, St. Peter the Apostle, Holy Childhood and the Missionary Union—have the common purpose of fostering a universal missionary spirit among the People of God. The Missionary Union has as its immediate and specific purpose the promotion of missionary consciousness and formation among priests and men and women religious, who in turn will provide this consciousness and formation within the Christian communities. In addition, the Missionary Union seeks to promote the other Societies, of which it is the "soul,"[168] "This must be our motto: All the churches united for the conversion of the whole world."[169]

Because they are under the auspices of the Pope and of the College of Bishops, these Societies, also within the boundaries of the particular churches, rightly have "the first place...since they are the means by which Catholics from their very infancy are imbued with a genuinely universal and missionary spirit; they are also the means which ensure an effective collection of resources for the good of all the missions, in accordance with the needs of each one."[170] Another purpose of the Missionary Societies is the fostering of lifelong vocations *ad gentes,* in both the older and younger churches. I earnestly recommend that their promotional work be increasingly directed to this goal.

In their activities, these Societies depend at the worldwide level on the Congregation for the Evangelization of Peoples; at the local level they depend on the Episcopal Conferences and the bishops of individual churches, in collaboration with existing promotional centers. They bring to the Catholic world that spirit of universality and of service to the Church's mission, without which authentic cooperation does not exist.

Not Only Giving to the Missions
But Receiving From Them As Well

85. Cooperating in missionary activity means not just giving but also receiving. All the particular churches, both young and old, are called to give and to receive in the context of the universal mission, and none should be closed to the needs of others. The Council states: "By virtue of...catholicity, the individual parts bring their own gifts to the other parts and to the whole Church, in such a way that the whole and individual parts grow greater through the mutual communication of all and their united efforts toward fullness in unity.... Between the different parts of the Church there are bonds of intimate communion with regard to spiritual riches, apostolic workers and temporal assistance."[171]

I exhort all the churches, and the bishops, priests, religious and members of the laity, to *be open to the Church's universality,* and to avoid every form of provincialism or exclusiveness, or feelings of self-sufficiency. Local churches, although rooted in their own people and their own culture, must always maintain an effective sense of the universality of the faith, giving and receiving spiritual gifts, experiences of pastoral work in evangelization and initial proclamation, as well as personnel for the apostolate and material resources.

The temptation to become isolated can be a strong one. The older churches, involved in new evangelization, may think that their mission is now at home, and thus they may risk slackening their drive toward the non-Christian world, begrudgingly conceding vocations to missionary institutes, religious congregations or other particular churches. But it is by giving generously of what we have that we will receive. Already the young churches, many of which are blessed with an abundance of vocations, are in a position to send priests and men and women religious to the older churches.

On the other hand, the young churches are concerned about their own identity, about inculturation, and about their freedom to grow independently of external influences, with the possible result that they close their doors to missionaries. To these churches I say: Do not isolate yourselves; willingly accept missionaries and support from other churches, and do likewise throughout the world. Precisely because of the problems that concern you, you need to be in continuous contact with your brothers and sisters in the faith. With every legitimate means, seek to ensure recognition of the freedom to which you have a right, remembering that Christ's disciples must "obey God rather than men" (Acts 5:29).

God Is Preparing a New Springtime for the Gospel

86. If we look at today's world, we are struck by many negative factors that can lead to pessimism. But this feeling is unjustified: we have faith in God our Father and Lord, in his goodness and mercy. As the third millennium of the redemption draws near, God is preparing a great springtime for Christianity, and we can already see its first signs. In fact, both in the non-Christian world and in the traditionally Christian world, people are gradually drawing closer to gospel ideals and values, a development which the Church seeks to encourage. Today in fact there is a new consensus among peoples about these values: the rejection of violence and war; respect for the human person and for human rights; the desire for freedom, justice and brotherhood; the surmounting of different forms of racism and nationalism; the affirmation of the dignity and role of women.

Christian hope sustains us in committing ourselves fully to the new evangelization and to the worldwide mission, and leads us to pray as Jesus taught us: "Thy Kingdom come. Thy will be done, on earth as it is in heaven" (Mt 6:10).

The number of those awaiting Christ is still immense: the human and cultural groups not yet reached by the Gospel, or for whom the Church is scarcely present, are so widespread as to require the uniting of all the Church's resources. As she prepares to celebrate the jubilee of the year 2000, the whole Church is even more committed to a new missionary advent. We must increase our apostolic zeal to pass on to others the light and joy of the faith, and to this high ideal the whole People of God must be educated.

We cannot be content when we consider the millions of our brothers and sisters, who like us have been redeemed by the blood of Christ, but who live in ignorance of the love of God. For each believer, as for the entire Church, the missionary task must remain foremost, for it concerns the eternal destiny of humanity and corresponds to God's mysterious and merciful plan.

Chapter VIII

Missionary Spirituality

87. Missionary activity demands a specific spirituality, which applies in particular to all those whom God has called to be missionaries.

Being Led by the Spirit

This spirituality is expressed first of all by a life of complete docility to the Spirit. It commits us to being molded from within by the Spirit, so that we may become ever more like Christ. It is not possible to bear witness to Christ without reflecting his image, which is made alive in us by grace and the power of the Spirit. This docility then commits us to receive the gifts of fortitude and discernment, which are essential elements of missionary spirituality.

An example of this is found with the apostles during the Master's public life. Despite their love for him and their generous response to his call, they proved to be incapable of understanding his words and reluctant to follow him along the path of suffering and humiliation. The Spirit transformed them into courageous witnesses to Christ and enlightened heralds of his word. It was the Spirit himself who guided them along the difficult and new paths of mission.

Today, as in the past, that mission is difficult and complex, and demands the courage and light of the Spirit. We often experience the dramatic situation of the first Christian community, which witnessed unbelieving and hostile forces "gathered together against the Lord and his Anointed" (Acts 4:26). Now, as then, we must pray that God will grant us boldness in preaching the Gospel; we must ponder the mysterious ways of the Spirit and allow ourselves to be led by him into all the truth (cf. Jn 16:13).

Living the Mystery of Christ, "the One who was sent"

88. An essential characteristic of missionary spirituality is intimate communion with Christ. We cannot understand or carry out the mission unless we refer it to Christ as the one who was sent to evangelize. St. Paul describes Christ's attitude: "Have this mind among yourselves, which is yours in Christ Jesus, who, though he was in the form of God, did not count equality with God a thing to be grasped, but emptied himself, taking the form of a servant, being born in the likeness of men. And being found in human form he humbled himself and became obedient unto death, even death on a cross" (Phil 2:5-8).

The mystery of the Incarnation and Redemption is thus described as a total self-emptying which leads Christ to experience fully the human condition and to accept totally the Father's plan. This is an emptying of self which is permeated by love and expresses love. The mission follows this same path and leads to the foot of the cross.

The missionary is required to "renounce himself and everything that up to this point he considered as his own, and to make himself everything to everyone."[172] This he does by a poverty which sets him free for the Gospel, overcoming attachment to the people and things about him, so that he may become a brother to those to whom he is sent and thus bring them Christ the Savior. This is the goal of missionary spirituality: "To the weak I became weak...; I have become all things to all men, that I might by all means save some. I do it all for the sake of the Gospel..." (1 Cor 9:22-23).

It is precisely because he is "sent" that the missionary experiences the consoling presence of Christ, who is with him at every moment of life—"Do not be afraid...for I am with you" (Acts 18:9-10)—and who awaits him in the heart of every person.

Loving the Church and Humanity As Jesus Did

89. Missionary spirituality is also marked by apostolic charity, the charity of Christ who came "to gather into one the children of God who are scattered abroad" (Jn 11:52), of the Good Shepherd who knows his sheep, who searches them out and offers his life for them (cf. Jn 10). Those who have the missionary spirit feel Christ's burning love for souls, and love the Church as Christ did.

The missionary is urged on by "zeal for souls," a zeal inspired by Christ's own charity, which takes the form of concern, tenderness, compassion, openness, availability and interest in people's problems. Jesus' love is very deep: he who "knew what was in man" (Jn 2:25) loved everyone by offering them redemption and suffered when it was rejected.

The missionary is a person of charity. In order to proclaim to all his brothers and sisters that they are loved by God and are capable of loving, he must show love toward all, giving his life for his neighbor. The missionary is the "universal brother," bearing in himself the Church's spirit, her openness to and interest in all peoples and individuals, especially the least and poorest of his brethren. As such, he overcomes barriers and divisions of race, cast or ideology. He is a sign of God's love in the world—a love without exclusion or partiality.

Finally, like Christ he must love the Church: "Christ loved

111

the Church and gave himself up for her" (Eph 5:25). This love, even to the point of giving one's life, is a focal point for him. Only profound love for the Church can sustain the missionary's zeal. His daily pressure, as St. Paul says, is "anxiety for all the churches" (2 Cor 11:28). For every missionary "fidelity to Christ cannot be separated from fidelity to the Church."[173]

The True Missionary Is the Saint

90. The call to mission derives, of its nature, from the call to holiness. A missionary is really such only if he commits himself to the way of holiness: "Holiness must be called a fundamental presupposition and an irreplaceable condition for everyone in fulfilling the mission of salvation in the Church."[174]

The universal call to holiness is closely linked to the *universal call to mission.* Every member of the faithful is called to holiness and to mission. This was the earnest desire of the Council, which hoped to be able "to enlighten all people with the brightness of Christ, which gleams over the face of the Church, by preaching the Gospel to every creature."[175] The Church's missionary spirituality is a journey toward holiness.

The renewed impulse to the mission *ad gentes* demands holy missionaries. It is not enough to update pastoral techniques, organize and coordinate ecclesial resources, or delve more deeply into the biblical and theological foundations of faith. What is needed is the encouragement of a new "ardor for holiness" among missionaries and throughout the Christian community, especially among those who work most closely with missionaries.[176]

Dear brothers and sisters: let us remember the missionary enthusiasm of the first Christian communities. Despite the limited means of travel and communication in those times, the proclamation of the Gospel quickly reached the ends of the earth. And this was the religion of a man who had died on a cross, "a stumbling block to Jews and folly to Gentiles"! (1 Cor 1:23) Underlying this missionary dynamism was the holiness of the first Christians and the first communities.

91. I therefore address myself to the recently baptized members of the young communities and young churches. Today, you are the hope of this two-thousand-year-old Church of ours: being young in faith, you must be like the first Christians and radiate enthusiasm and courage, in generous devotion to God and neighbor. In a word, you must set yourselves on the path of holiness. Only thus can you be a sign of God in the world and re-live in your own countries the missionary epic of the early Church. You will also be a leaven of missionary spirit for the older churches.

For their part, missionaries should reflect on the duty of holiness required of them by the gift of their vocation, renew themselves in spirit day by day, and strive to update their doctrinal and pastoral formation. The missionary must be a "contemplative in action." He finds answers to problems in the light of God's word and in personal and community prayer. My contact with representatives of the non-Christian spiritual traditions, particularly those of Asia, has confirmed me in the view that the future of mission depends to a great extent on contemplation. Unless the missionary is a contemplative he cannot proclaim Christ in a credible way. He is a witness to the experience of God, and must be able to say with the apostles: "that which we have looked upon...concerning the word of life,...we proclaim also to you" (1 Jn 1:1-3).

The missionary is a person of the Beatitudes. Before sending out the Twelve to evangelize, Jesus, in his "missionary discourse" (cf. Mt 10), teaches them the paths of mission:

poverty, meekness, acceptance of suffering and persecution, the desire for justice and peace, charity—in other words, the Beatitudes, lived out in the apostolic life (cf. Mt 5:1-12). By living the Beatitudes, the missionary experiences and shows concretely that the kingdom of God has already come, and that he has accepted it. The characteristic of every authentic missionary life is the inner joy that comes from faith. In a world tormented and oppressed by so many problems, a world tempted to pessimism, the one who proclaims the "Good News" must be a person who has found true hope in Christ.

Conclusion

92. Today, as never before, the Church has the opportunity of bringing the Gospel, by witness and word, to all people and nations. I see the dawning of a new missionary age, which will become a radiant day bearing an abundant harvest, if all Christians, and missionaries and young churches in particular, respond with generosity and holiness to the calls and challenges of our time.

Like the apostles after Christ's Ascension, the Church must gather in the Upper Room "together with Mary, the Mother of Jesus" (Acts 1:14), in order to pray for the Spirit and to gain strength and courage to carry out the missionary mandate. We too, like the apostles, need to be transformed and guided by the Spirit.

On the eve of the third millennium the whole Church is invited to live more intensely the mystery of Christ by gratefully cooperating in the work of salvation. The Church does this together with Mary and following the example of Mary, the Church's Mother and model: Mary is the model of that maternal love which should inspire all who cooperate in the Church's apostolic mission for the rebirth of humanity. Therefore, "strengthened by the presence of Christ, the Church journeys through time toward the consummation of the ages and goes to meet the Lord who comes. But on this journey ...she proceeds along *the path* already trodden by the Virgin Mary."[177]

To "Mary's mediation, wholly oriented toward Christ and

tending to the revelation of his salvific power,"[178] I entrust the Church and, in particular, those who commit themselves to carrying out the missionary mandate in today's world. As Christ sent forth his apostles in the name of the Father and of the Son and of the Holy Spirit, so too, renewing that same mandate, I extend to all of you my apostolic blessing, in the name of the same Most Holy Trinity. Amen.

Given in Rome, at St. Peter's, on December 7, the twenty-fifth anniversary of the Conciliar Decree *Ad Gentes,* in the year 1990, the thirteenth of my Pontificate.

Joannes Paulus PP. II

Notes

1. Cf. Paul VI, Message for World Mission Day, 1972, *Insegnamenti X,* (1972), 522: "How many internal tensions, which weaken and divide certain local churches and institutions, would disappear before the firm conviction that the salvation of local communities is procured through cooperation in work for the spread of the Gospel to the farthest bounds of the earth!"

2. Cf. Benedict XV, Apostolic Letter *Maximum Illud* (November 30, 1919): *AAS* 11 (1919), 440-455; Pius XI, Enclyclical Letter *Rerum Ecclesiae* (February 28, 1926): *AAS* 18 (1926), 65-83; Pius XII, Encyclical *Letter Evangelii Praecones* (June 2, 1951): *AAS* 43 (1951), 497-528; Encyclical Letter *Fidei Donum* (April 21, 1957): *AAS* 49 (1957), 225-248; John XXIII, Encyclical Letter *Princeps Pastorum* (November 28, 1959): *AAS* 51 (1959), 833-864.

3. Encyclical Letter *Redemptor Hominis* (March 4, 1979), 10: *AAS* 71 (1979), 274f.

4. Ibid.: *loc. cit.,* 275.

5. Nicene-Constantinopolitan Creed: *DS* 150.

6. Encyclical Letter *Redemptor Hominis,* 13: *loc. cit.,* 283.

7. Cf. Second Vatican Ecumenical Council, Pastoral Constitution on the Church in the Modern World *Gaudium et Spes,* 2.

8. Ibid., 22.

9. Encyclical Letter *Dives in Misericordia* (November 30, 1980), 7: *AAS* 72 (1980), 1202.

10. *Homily* for the celebration of the Eucharist in Krakow, June 10, 1979: *AAS* 71 (1979), 873.

11. Cf. John XXIII, Encyclical Letter *Mater et Magistra* (May 15, 1961) IV *AAS* 53 (1961), 453.

12. Declaration on Religious Freedom *Dignitatis Humanae,* 2.

13. Paul VI, Apostolic Exhortation *Evangelii Nuntiandi* (December 8, 1975), 53: *AAS* 68 (1976), 42.

14. Declaration on Religious Freedom *Dignitatis Humanae,* 2.

15. Cf. Dogmatic Constitution on the Church *Lumen Gentium,* 14-17; Decree on the Missionary Activity of the Church *Ad Gentes,* 3.

16. Cf. Dogmatic Constitution on the Church *Lumen Gentium,* 48; Pastoral Constitution on the Church in the Modern World *Gaudium et Spes,* 43;

Decree on the Missionary Activity of the Church *Ad Gentes,* 7, 21.

17. Dogmatic Constitution on the Church *Lumen Gentium,* 13.

18. Ibid., 9.

19. Pastoral Constitution on the Church in the Modern World *Gaudium et Spes,* 22.

20. Second Vatican Ecumenical Council, Dogmatic Constitution on the Church, *Lumen Gentium,* 14.

21. Encyclical Letter *Dives in Misericordia,* 1: *loc. cit.,* 1177.

22. Second Vatican Ecumenical Council, Dogmatic Constitution on the Church *Lumen Gentium,* 5.

23. Cf. Second Vatican Ecumenical Council, Pastoral Constitution on the Church in the Modern World *Gaudium et Spes,* 22.

24. Cf. Second Vatican Ecumenical Council, Dogmatic Constitution on the Church *Lumen Gentium,* 4.

25. Ibid., 5.

26. Apostolic Exhortation *Evangelii Nuntiandi,* 16: *loc. cit.,* 15.

27. *Address* at the opening of the Third Session of the Second Vatican Ecumenical Council, September 14, 1964: *AAS* 56 (1964), 810.

28. Cf. Paul VI, Apostolic Exhortation *Evangelii Nuntiandi,* 34: *loc. cit.,* 28.

29. Cf. International Theological Commission, Select Themes of Ecclesiology on the Occasion of the Twentieth Anniversary of the Closing of the Second Vatican Council (October 7, 1985), 10: "The Eschatological Character of the Church: Kingdom and Church."

30. Cf. Second Vatican Ecumenical Council, Pastoral Constitution on the Church in the Modern World *Gaudium et Spes,* 39.

31. Encyclical Letter *Dominum et Vivificantem* (May 18, 1986), 42: *AAS* 78 (1986), 857.

32. Ibid., 64: *loc. cit.,* 892.

33. The Greek word "parrhesia" also means enthusiasm or energy; cf. Acts 2:29; 4:13, 29, 31; 9:27-28; 13:46; 14:3; 18:26; 19:8, 26; 28:31.

34. Cf. Paul VI, Apostolic Exhortation *Evangelii Nuntiandi,* 41-42: *loc. cit.,* 31-33.

35. Cf. Encyclical Letter *Dominum et Vivificantem,* 53: *loc. cit.,* 874f.

36. Cf. Second Vatican Ecumenical Council, Decree on the Missionary Activity of the Church *Ad Gentes,* 3, 11, 15; Pastoral Constitution on the Church in the Modern World *Gaudium et Spes,* 10-11, 22, 26, 38, 41, 92-93.

37. Second Vatican Ecumenical Council, Pastoral Constitution on the Church in the Modern World *Gaudium et Spes,* 10, 15, 22.

38. Ibid., 41.

39. Cf. Encyclical Letter *Dominum et Vivificantem,* 54: *loc. cit.,* 875f.

40. Second Vatican Ecumenical Council, Pastoral Constitution on the Church in the Modern World *Gaudium et Spes,* 26.

41. Ibid., 38; cf. 93.

42. Cf. Second Vatican Ecumenical Council, Dogmatic Constitution on the Church *Lumen Gentium,* 17; Decree on the Missionary Activity of the Church *Ad Gentes,* 3, 15.

43. Second Vatican Ecumenical Council, Decree on the Missionary Activity of the Church *Ad Gentes,* 4.

44. Cf. Encyclical Letter *Dominum et Vivificantem,* 53: *loc. cit.,* 874.

45. *Address* to Representatives of Non-Christian Religions, Madras, February 5, 1986: *AAS* 78 (1986), 767; cf. *Message to the Peoples of Asia,* Manila, February 21, 1981, 2-4: *AAS* 73 (1981), 392f; *Address* to Representatives of Other Religions, Tokyo, February 24, 1981, 3-4: *Insegnamenti* IV/I (1981), 507f.

46. *Address* to Cardinals and the Roman Curia, December 22, 1986, 11: *AAS* 79 (1987), 1089.

47. Cf. Second Vatican Ecumenical Council, Dogmatic Constitution on the Church *Lumen Gentium,* 16.

48. Second Vatican Ecumenical Council, Pastoral Constitution on the Church in the Modern World *Gaudium et Spes,* 45; cf. Encyclical Letter *Dominum et Vivificantem,* 54: *loc. cit.,* 876.

49. Second Vatican Ecumenical Council, Decree on the Missionary Activity of the Church *Ad Gentes,* 10.

50. Apostolic Exhortation *Christifideles Laici* (December 30, 1988), 35: *AAS* 81 (1989), 457.

51. Cf. Second Vatican Ecumenical Council, Decree on the Missionary Activity of the Church *Ad Gentes,* 6.

52. Cf. ibid.

53. Cf. ibid., 6, 23, 27.

54. Cf. Paul VI, Apostolic Exhortation *Evangelii Nuntiandi,* 18-20: *loc. cit.,* 17-19.

55. Apostolic Exhortation *Christifideles Laici,* 35: *loc. cit.,* 457.

56. Apostolic Exhortation *Evangelii Nuntiandi,* 80: *loc. cit.,* 73.

57. Cf. Second Vatican Ecumenical Council, Decree on the Missionary Activity of the Church *Ad Gentes,* 6.

58. Apostolic Exhortation *Evangelii Nuntiandi,* 80: *loc. cit.,* 73.

59. Cf. Decree on the Missionary Activity of the Church *Ad Gentes,* 6.

60. Cf. ibid, 20.

61. Cf. *Address* to the members of the Symposium of the Council of the European Episcopal Conferences, October 11, 1985: *AAS* 78 (1986), 178-189.

62. Apostolic Exhortation *Evangelii Nuntiandi,* 20: *loc. cit.,* 19.

63. Second Vatican Ecumenical Council, Decree on the Missionary Activity of the Church *Ad Gentes,* 5; cf. Dogmatic Constitution on the Church *Lumen Gentium,* 8.

64. Cf. Second Vatican Ecumenical Council, Declaration on Religious Freedom *Dignitatis Humanae,* 3-4; Paul VI, Apostolic Exhortation *Evangelii Nuntiandi,* 79-80: *loc. cit.,* 71-75; John Paul II, Encyclical Letter *Redemptor Hominis,* 12: *loc. cit.,* 278-281.

65. Apostolic Letter *Maximum Illud: loc. cit.,* 446.

66. Paul VI, Apostolic Exhortation *Evangelii Nuntiandi,* 62: *loc. cit.,* 52.

67. Cf. *De praescriptione haereticorum,* XX: *CCL,* I, 201f.

68. Second Vatican Ecumenical Council, Decree on the Missionary Activity of the Church *Ad Gentes,* 9; cf. Chapter II, 10-18.

69. Cf. Paul VI, Apostolic Exhortation *Evangelii Nuntiandi,* 41: *loc. cit.,* 31f.

70. Cf. Second Vatican Ecumenical Council, Dogmatic Constitution on the Church *Lumen Gentium,* 28, 35, 38; Pastoral Constitution on the Church in the Modern World *Gaudium et Spes,* 43; Decree on the Missionary Activity of the Church *Ad Gentes,* 11-12.

71. Cf. Paul VI, Encyclical Letter *Populorum Progressio* (March 26, 1967), 21, 42: *AAS* 59 (1967), 267f, 278.

72. Paul VI, Apostolic Exhortation *Evangelii Nuntiandi,* 27: *loc. cit.,* 23.

73. Second Vatican Ecumenical Council, Decree on the Missionary Activity of the Church *Ad Gentes,* 13.

74. Cf. Paul VI, Apostolic Exhortation *Evangelii Nuntiandi,* 15: *loc. cit.,* 13-15; Second Vatican Ecumenical Council, Decree on the Missionary Activity of the Church *Ad Gentes,* 13-14.

75. Cf. Encyclical Letter *Dominum et Vivificantem,* 42, 64: *loc. cit.,* 857-859, 892-894.

76. Cf. Paul VI, Apostolic Exhortation *Evangelii Nuntiandi,* 60: *loc. cit.,* 50f.

77. Cf. Second Vatican Ecumenical Council, Dogmatic Constitution on the Church *Lumen Gentium,* 6-9.

78. Second Vatican Ecumenical Council, Decree on the Missionary Activity of the Church *Ad Gentes,* 2; cf. Dogmatic Constitution on the Church *Lumen Gentium,* 9.

79. Cf. Decree on the Missionary Activity of the Church *Ad Gentes,* Chapter III, 19-22.

80. Ibid., 15.

81. Ibid., 6.

82. Ibid., 15; cf. Decree on Ecumenism *Unitatis Redintegratio,* 3.

83. Cf. Apostolic Exhortation *Evangelii Nuntiandi,* 58: *loc. cit.,* 46-49.

84. Extraordinary Assembly of 1985, *Final Report,* II, C, 6.

85. Ibid., II, D, 4.

86. Cf. Apostolic Exhortation *Catechesi Tradendae* (October 16, 1979), 53: *AAS* 71 (1979), 1320; Encyclical Epistle *Slavorum Apostoli* (June 2, 1985), 21: *AAS* 77 (1985), 802f.

87. Cf. Paul VI, Apostolic Exhortation *Evangelii Nuntiandi*, 20: *loc. cit.*, 18f.

88. *Address* to the Bishops of Zaire, Kinshasa, May 3, 1980, 4-6: *AAS* 72 (1980), 432-435; *Address* to the Bishops of Kenya, Nairobi, May 7, 1980, 6: *AAS* 72 (1980), 497; *Address* to the Bishops of India, Delhi, February 1, 1986, 5: *AAS* 78 (1986), 748f; *Homily* at Cartagena, July 6, 1986, 7-8: *AAS* 79 (1987), 105f; cf. also Encyclical Epistle *Slavorum Apostoli*, 21-22; *loc. cit.*, 802-804.

89. Cf. Second Vatican Ecumenical Council, Decree on the Missionary Activity of the Church *Ad Gentes*, 22.

90. Cf. ibid.

91. Cf. Paul VI, Apostolic Exhortation *Evangelii Nuntiandi*, 64: *loc. cit.*, 55.

92. Ibid., 63: *loc. cit.*, 53: Particular Churches "have the task of assimilating the essence of the Gospel message and of transposing it, without the slightest betrayal of its essential truth, into the language that these people understand, then of proclaiming it in this language.... And the word 'language' should be understood here less in the semantic or literary sense than in the sense which one may call anthropological or cultural."

93. Cf. *Address* at the General Audience of April 13, 1988: *Insegnamenti* XI/I (1988), 877-881.

94. Apostolic Exhortation *Familiaris Consortio*, (November 22, 1981), 10: *AAS* 74 (1982), 91, which speaks of inculturation "in the context of marriage and the family."

95. Cf. Paul VI, Apostolic Exhortation *Evangelii Nuntiandi*, 63-65: *loc. cit.*, 53-56.

96. Second Vatican Ecumenical Council, Dogmatic Constitution on the Church *Lumen Gentium*, 17.

97. *Address* to those participating in the Symposium of African Bishops at Kampala, July 31, 1969, 2: *AAS* 61 (1969), 577.

98. Paul VI, *Address* at the opening of the Second Session of the Second Vatican Ecumenical Council, September 29, 1963: *AAS* 55 (1963), 858; cf. Second Vatican Ecumenical Council, Declaration on the Church's Relation to Non-Christian Religions *Nostra Aetate*, 2; Dogmatic Constitution on the Church *Lumen Gentium*, 16; Decree on the Missionary Activity of the Church *Ad Gentes*, 9; Paul VI, Apostolic Exhortation *Evangelii Nuntiandi*, 53: *loc. cit.* 41f.

99. Cf. Paul VI, Encyclical Letter *Ecclesiam Suam* (August 6, 1964): *AAS* 56 (1964), 609-659; Second Vatican Ecumenical Council, Decree on the Missionary Activity of the Church *Ad Gentes*, 11, 41; Secretariat for Non-Christians, Document *L'atteggiamento della Chiesa di fronte ai seguaci di altre religioni:* Riflessioni e orientamenti su dialogo e missione (September 4, 1984): *AAS* 76 (1984), 816-828.

100. *Letter* to the Fifth Plenary Assembly of Asian Bishops' Conferences (June 23, 1990), 4: *L'Osservatore Romano*, July 18, 1990.

101. Second Vatican Ecumenical Council, Dogmatic Constitution on the Church *Lumen Gentium,* 14; cf. Decree on the Missionary Activity of the Church *Ad Gentes,* 7.

102. Cf. Second Vatican Ecumenical Council, Decree on Ecumenism *Unitatis Redintegratio,* 3; Decree on the Missionary Activity of the Church *Ad Gentes,* 7.

103. Cf. Encyclical Letter *Redemptor Hominis,* 12: *loc. cit.,* 279.

104. Second Vatican Ecumenical Council, Decree on the Missionary Activity of the Church *Ad Gentes,* 11, 15.

105. Second Vatican Ecumenical Council, Declaration on the Church's Relation to Non-Christian Religions *Nostra Aetate,* 2.

106. Apostolic Exhortation *Christifideles Laici,* 35: *loc. cit.,* 458.

107. Cf. Second Vatican Ecumenical Council, Decree on the Missionary Activity of the Church *Ad Gentes,* 41.

108. Encyclical Letter *Sollicitudo Rei Socialis* (December 30, 1987), 41: *AAS* 80 (1988), 570f.

109. *Documents* of the Third General Conference of Latin American Bishops, Puebla (1979), 3760 (1145).

110. *Address* to Clergy and Religious, Jakarta, October 10, 1989, 5: *L'Osservatore Romano,* October 11, 1989.

111. Cf. Paul VI, Encyclical Letter *Populorum Progressio,* 14-21, 40-42: *loc. cit.,* 264-268, 277f; John Paul II, Encyclical Letter *Sollicitudo Rei Socialis,* 27-41: *loc. cit.,* 547-572.

112. Cf. Encyclical Letter *Sollicitudo Rei Socialis,* 28: *loc. cit.,* 548-550.

113. Cf. ibid., Chapter IV, 27-34: *loc. cit.,* 547-560; Paul VI, Encyclical Letter *Populorum Progressio,* 19-21, 41-42: *loc. cit.,* 266-268, 277f.

114. *Address* to the residents of "Favela Vidigal" in Rio de Janeiro, July 2, 1980, 4: *AAS* 72 (1980), 854.

115. *Documents* of the Third General Conference of Latin American Bishops, Puebla, (1979), 3757 (1142).

116. Isaac of Stella, *Sermon* 31, *PL* 194, 1793.

117. Second Vatican Ecumenical Council, Decree on the Missionary Activity of the Church *Ad Gentes,* 20.

118. Apostolic Exhortation *Christifideles Laici,* 35: *loc. cit.,* 458.

119. Cf. Second Vatican Ecumenical Council, Decree on the Missionary Activity of the Church *Ad Gentes,* 38.

120. *Address* to Cardinals and those associated in the work of the Roman Curia, Vatican City and the Vicariate of Rome, June 28, 1980, 10: *Insegnamenti,* III/1 (1980), 1887.

121. Dogmatic Constitution on the Church *Lumen Gentium,* 23.

122. Decree on the Missionary Activity of the Church *Ad Gentes,* 38.

123. Ibid., 29.

124. Cf. ibid., 38.

125. Ibid., 30.

126. *Documents* of the Third General Conference of Latin American Bishops, Puebla (1979): 2941 (368).

127. Cf. Norms for the Cooperation of the Local Churches Among Themselves and especially for a Better Distribution of the Clergy in the World *Postquam Apostoli* (March 25, 1980): *AAS* 72 (1980), 343-364.

128. Cf. Decree on the Missionary Activity of the Church *Ad Gentes*, Chapter IV, 23-27.

129. Ibid., 23.

130. Ibid.

131. Ibid., 23, 27.

132. Cf. Sacred Congregation for Religious and Secular Institutes and Sacred Congregation for Bishops, Directives for Mutual Relations between Bishops and Religious in the Church *Mutuae Relationes* (May 14, 1978), 14b: *AAS* 70 (1978), 482; cf. n. 28: *loc. cit.*, 490.

133. Second Vatican Ecumenical Council, Decree on the Missionary Activity of the Church *Ad Gentes*, 27.

134. Second Vatican Ecumenical Council, Decree on the Ministry and Life of Priests *Presbyterorum Ordinis*, 10; cf. Decree on the Missionary Activity of the Church *Ad Gentes*, 39.

135. Second Vatican Ecumenical Council, Decree on Priestly Formation *Optatam Totius*, 20: cf. "Guide de la vie pastorale pour les prêtres diocésains des Eglises qui dependent de la Congrégation pour l'Evangélisation des Peuples," Rome, 1989.

136. *Address* to the Plenary Assembly of the Congregation for the Evangelization of Peoples, April 14, 1989, 4: *AAS* 81 (1989), 1140.

137. *Message* for World Mission Day, 1982: *Insegnamenti* V/2 (1982), 1879.

138. Cf. Second Vatican Ecumenical Council, Decree on the Missionary Activity of the Church *Ad Gentes*, 38; Sacred Congregation for the Clergy, Norms *Postquam Apostoli*, 24-25: *loc. cit.*, 361.

139. Cf. Sacred Congregation for the Clergy, Norms *Postquam Apostoli*, 29: *loc. cit.*, 362f; Second Vatican Ecumenical Council, Decree on the Missionary Activity of the Church *Ad Gentes*, 20.

140. *CIC*, c. 783.

141. Decree on the Missionary Activity of the Church *Ad Gentes*, 40.

142. Cf. Paul VI, Apostolic Exhortation *Evangelii Nuntiandi*, 69: *loc. cit.*, 58f.

143. Apostolic Letter *Mulieris Dignitatem* (August 15, 1988), 20: *AAS* 80 (1988), 1703.

144. Cf. Pius XII, Encyclical Letter *Evangelii Praecones: loc. cit.*, 510ff; Encyclical Letter *Fidei Donum: loc. cit.*, 228ff; John XXIII, Encyclical Letter *Princeps Pastorum: loc. cit.*, 855ff; Paul VI, Apostolic Exhortation *Evangelii*

Nuntiandi, 70-73: *loc. cit.,* 59-63.

145. Apostolic Exhortation *Christifideles Laici,* 35: *loc. cit.,* 457.

146. Cf. Encyclical Letter *Evangelii Praecones: loc. cit.,* 510-514.

147. Cf. Dogmatic Constitution on the Church *Lumen Gentium,* 17, 33ff.

148. Cf. Decree on the Missionary Activity of the Church *Ad Gentes,* 35-36, 41.

149. Apostolic Exhortation *Christifideles Laici,* 14: *loc. cit.,* 410.

150. *CIC,* c. 225, 1; cf. Second Vatican Ecumenical Council, Decree on the Apostolate of the Laity *Apostolicam Actuositatem,* 6, 13.

151. Second Vatican Ecumenical Council, Dogmatic Constitution on the Church *Lumen Gentium,* 31; cf. *CIC,* c. 225, 2.

152. Paul VI, Apostolic Exhortation *Evangelii Nuntiandi,* 70: *loc. cit.,* 60.

153. Apostolic Exhortation *Christifideles Laici,* 35: *loc. cit.,* 458.

154. Second Vatican Ecumenical Council, Decree on the Missionary Activity of the Church *Ad Gentes,* 17.

155. Apostolic Exhortation *Catechesi Tradendae,* 66: *loc. cit.,* 1331.

156. Cf. c. 785, 1.

157. Decree on the Missionary Activity of the Church *Ad Gentes,* 17.

158. Cf. Plenary Assembly of the Sacred Congregation for the Evangelization of Peoples, 1969, on catechists, and the related "Instruction" of April 1970: *Bibliographia Missionaria* 34 (1970), 197-212 and *S.C. de Propaganda Fide Memoria Rerum,* III/2 (1976), 821-831.

159. Second Vatican Ecumenical Council, Decree on the Missionary Activity of the Church *Ad Gentes,* 28.

160. Apostolic Constitution *Pastor Bonus* (June 28, 1988), 85: *AAS* 80 (1988), 881; cf. Second Vatican Ecumenical Council, Decree on the Missionary Activity of the Church *Ad Gentes,* 29.

161. Second Vatican Ecumenical Council, Decree on the Missionary Activity of the Church *Ad Gentes,* 29: Cf. John Paul II, Apostolic Constitution *Pastor Bonus,* 86: *loc. cit.,* 882.

162. Decree on the Missionary Activity of the Church *Ad Gentes,* 31.

163. Cf. ibid., 33.

164. Cf. Paul VI, Apostolic Letter Motu Proprio *Ecclesiae Sanctae* (August 6, 1966), II, 43: *AAS* 58 (1966), 782.

165. Cf. Second Vatican Ecumenical Council, Decree on the Missionary Activity of the Church *Ad Gentes,* 34; Paul VI, Apostolic Letter Motu Proprio *Ecclesiae Sanctae,* III, 22: *loc. cit.,* 787.

166. Second Vatican Ecumenical Council, Decree on the Missionary Activity of the Church *Ad Gentes,* 35; cf. *CIC,* cc. 211, 781.

167. Apostolic Exhortation *Familiaris Consortio,* 54: *loc. cit.,* 147.

168. Cf. Paul VI, Apostolic Epistle *Graves et Increscentes* (September 5, 1966): *AAS* 58 (1966), 750-756.

169. P. Manna, *Le nostre "Chiese" e la propagazione del Vangelo*, Trentola Ducenta, 1952[2], p. 35.

170. Second Vatican Ecumenical Council, Decree on the Missionary Activity of the Church *Ad Gentes*, 38.

171. Dogmatic Constitution on the Church *Lumen Gentium*, 13.

172. Second Vatican Ecumenical Council, Decree on the Missionary Activity of the Church *Ad Gentes*, 24.

173. Second Vatican Ecumenical Council, Decree on the Ministry and Life of Priests *Presbyterorum Ordinis*, 14.

174. Apostolic Exhortation *Christifideles Laici*, 17: *loc. cit.*, 419.

175. Dogmatic Constitution on the Church *Lumen Gentium*, 1.

176. Cf. *Address* at CELAM Meeting, Port-au-Prince, March 9, 1983: *AAS* 75 (1983), 771-779; *Homily* for the Opening of the "Novena of Years" promoted by CELAM, Santo Domingo, October 12, 1984: *Insegnamenti* VII/2 (1984), 885-897.

177. Encyclical Letter *Redemptoris Mater* (March 25, 1987), 2: *AAS* 79 (1987), 362f.

178. Ibid., 22: *loc. cit.*, 390.

BOOKS & MEDIA

The Daughters of St. Paul operate book and media centers at the following addresses. Visit, call or write the one nearest you today, or find us on the World Wide Web, www.pauline.org

California
3908 Sepulveda Blvd., Culver City, CA 90230; 310-397-8676
5945 Balboa Ave., San Diego, CA 92111; 619-565-9181
46 Geary Street, San Francisco, CA 94108; 415-781-5180

Florida
145 S.W. 107th Ave., Miami, FL 33174; 305-559-6715

Hawaii
1143 Bishop Street, Honolulu, HI 96813; 808-521-2731
Neighbor Islands call: 800-259-8463

Illinois
172 North Michigan Ave., Chicago, IL 60601; 312-346-4228

Louisiana
4403 Veterans Memorial Blvd., Metairie, LA 70006; 504-887-7631

Massachusetts
Rte. 1, 885 Providence Hwy., Dedham, MA 02026; 781-326-5385

Missouri
9804 Watson Rd., St. Louis, MO 63126; 314-965-3512

New Jersey
561 U.S. Route 1, Wick Plaza, Edison, NJ 08817; 732-572-1200

New York
150 East 52nd Street, New York, NY 10022; 212-754-1110
78 Fort Place, Staten Island, NY 10301; 718-447-5071

Ohio
2105 Ontario Street, Cleveland, OH 44115; 216-621-9427

Pennsylvania
9171-A Roosevelt Blvd., Philadelphia, PA 19114; 215-676-9494

South Carolina
243 King Street, Charleston, SC 29401; 843-577-0175

Tennessee
4811 Poplar Ave., Memphis, TN 38117; 901-761-2987

Texas
114 Main Plaza, San Antonio, TX 78205; 210-224-8101

Virginia
1025 King Street, Alexandria, VA 22314; 703-549-3806

Canada
3022 Dufferin Street, Toronto, Ontario, Canada M6B 3T5; 416-781-9131
1155 Yonge Street, Toronto, Ontario, Canada M4T 1W2; 416-934-3440

¡Libros en español!